LIFE/DEATH RHYTHMS OF CAPITALIST REGIMES – DEBT BEFORE DISHONOUR

LIFE/DEATH RHYTHMS OF CAPITALIST REGIMES – DEBT BEFORE DISHONOUR

Timetable of World Dominance 1400 to 2100 AD

PART I   HISTORICAL RULER CYCLES

WILL SLATYER

PARTRIDGE
A Penguin Random House Company

To order additional copies of this book, contact
Toll Free 800 101 2657 (Singapore)
Toll Free 1 800 81 7340 (Malaysia)
orders.singapore@partridgepublishing.com

www.partridgepublishing.com/singapore

CONTENTS

PREFACE

In the 1980s I developed a system of financial risk management from my philosophy that capitalism was a socially accepted form of warfare that banking organisations used to dominate the twentieth century. In the twentieth century, debt had become a necessary tool of capitalist warfare. My risk management consultancy allowed the modern international corporation to manage debt in a computerised world where huge sums of money move instantaneously from country to country. I also used financial cycles as a background to financial management and looked to history to provide further knowledge of human cycles. I was unable to find one book on history that provided a flow of history over an extended period that would allow long term cyclical analysis. Having basically retired from financial management, I have written books as the first attempts to provide the historical basis for understanding of age-old human nature, which then can be used to recognise present and future changes in societies.

I am not a classically trained historian, but a market technical analyst and risk manager who has learned over many years that the economic affairs of nations and corporations follow patterns of human nature, often associated with varying degrees of greed and fear. Human nature has changed little in 5000 years. Religion, debt and war are as relevant today, as they were in the Babylonian kingdom of Hammurabi in 1750BC. All the advanced computerised technology of the twenty-first century international monetary system is operated and directed, by men who have the same emotions of greed and fear as the men who used primitive weapons to achieve ancient economic domination. My first book - "**Life/Death Rhythms of Ancient Empires** - Predictable Climatic Cycles Influence War, Prosperity, Debt, Religion and Rule" described the ancient cycles 3000BC – 1400AD. In this book I shall endeavour to convince the reader that group dynamic patterns of history earlier identified, present a similar pattern after 1400AD that can be recognised and applied to the long term analysis of modern governments.

My historical reporting has been selected from many written sources which expanded exponentially during my research when I found that a number of academic authors disagreed with others over the truth of history. I have listed these sources in the bibliography, and whom I thank for their research and writing. I make no apology for the lack of footnotes referring individually to those sources, particularly since individual comments are immaterial to the cyclical theory. I have found from my experience with footnotes that they are often used as a spotlight to illuminate only the area which suits the opinion of the writer, without bringing to light other aspects of the source that might raise doubts. Where academics disagreed marginally, I have taken what I believe was the most logical view. When major controversial sources have been mentioned, I have noted the differences from orthodox academic opinion. I am especially indebted to Wikipedia which allowed me to précis long historical periods. Wikipedia information has been supported by historical sources. I apologise to friends and family for the long periods of isolation while carrying out research without much contact with the outside world.

My extensive general research has led me to believe that, in the modern era, there is not too much scope for original ideas to be presented today, simply new ways of understanding and implementing earlier philosophies using new technology. I will be giving my interpretation of recorded events, and possibly in a different context to some academic scholars, but shall not claim to have generated many enlightened or original ideas. In producing any new concepts in this book, I have been simply guided by wise men of past ages, and recognised their wisdom as being still relevant today, in the context of most recent technology.

The proper word throughout history for debt has been "usury", but this word has grown into misuse because the modern financial world cannot exist without usury. It has been commonly thought that debt had its origins with the coming of money. Debt in fact preceded invention of coinage, generally ascribed to the Lydians in the 7th century BC, by thousands of years. I demonstrated in my first book that societies have used debt, abused debt, revolted and warred over debt, and have forbidden usury, for much of human history. Since 1400, governments have found new ways to expand debt to produce modern economies, which are still subject to the age-old basic principle of debt – that it needs to be repaid or dire consequences ensue.

In this book I have outlined the dominant cultures that influenced often older or more passive cultures so that society evolved towards modern capitalism.

I believe my history validates the cyclical theory of my previous book that cultural progress occurred in waves to make up an identified cycle. If one accepts this cycle, the projections through the present can be used to forecast the likely cultural progress in future ages. More importantly I have confirmed the cycle of dominant cultures that have had major influences on the world. This cycle can be used to forecast lifetimes of future dominant cultures. I have forecast the timing and beginning of the next dominant culture.

It has been necessary, because of the cyclical reference to include many dates and names to identify the historical periods. I apologise if this irritates those who prefer the narrative style without many identifiable years. I hope that these people will treat the dates and names as simple signposts that, like the mile-posts on a road journey, can be noticed consciously only when one needs a reference, but ignored for most of the journey.

Will Slatyer 2014

PART I

Historical Ruler Cycles

CHAPTER 1

Periodic Behaviour of Human Societies and Climatic Cycles

"Those who cannot remember the past are condemned to repeat it."
George Santayana (1863 - 1952)

The goal of my exhaustive research since the 1980s has been to establish that there has been a discernible pattern to the growth of diverse world cultures over millennia, which make history dynamic in the present day. A secondary aim is to find a pattern in the evolution of capitalism that will be of benefit in the future. In my previous book, *Ebbs and Flows of Ancient Empires,* I outlined a template of cultural behaviour that had been followed by ancient dominant cultures 2500 BC–AD 1400. There were definite cycles of dominant, just, and prosperous cultures. Late in the period, there were signs of democracy in Greek Athens and the Roman Republic that did not survive military imperialism. That phase in human history was too early to discuss an actual capitalist system, even if some of the seeds had already been sown.

The period of history covered in this book, AD 1400–2100, will present the framework of history in order to identify the dominant culture over global geographic regions in any given period of time. I do not offer any apology that my understanding of dominant cultures might be different from that of some historical scholars. It appears to me from literary research that each academic scholar has produced his or her version of the truth, gleaned from records with more emphasis on historical figures and events filtered through the prevailing culture of the author.

I define *culture* as being a natural way of life in which activities, distinctive to a particular society, are unconsciously accepted by the people in that society as normal behaviour. Eating raw fish is natural in the Japanese culture, as is drinking fermented mare's milk in the Mongolian culture. Neither of these actions is natural in the American culture, where eating a huge slab of meat, undercooked from the rear end of a castrated bull, is commonplace. The Australian barbecue of the slab of meat is also natural in the southern continent but is basically alien to the English weather and culture which was dominant in the world when the Australian culture was born.

This book would be of no use to practical men if it were only a chronological history of historical cultures, without presenting lessons that can be learned to advantage from that history, in the present day and for the future. I hope to demonstrate in this book the possibility that a dominant culture, whether that of city/state, nation, or corporation, produces similar phases of behaviour throughout the long course of time.

There is also the possibility that societies of men have been stimulated into action by natural phenomena, in particular, changes in climate. There have been great prehistoric cataclysms, like the volcanic eruption that destroyed the Cretan island of Thera c1628 BC, that have caused huge disruptions to human society. The movement of Scandinavian tribes south around the sixth and seventh centuries BC was apparently due to a mini-ice age which made life above the Arctic Circle intolerable. Cold weather stimulated the migration of Cimbrians from Jutland circa 120 BC. The Germanic tribes moved south and west circa AD 400, again due to a severe cold climate which froze the Rhine.

I shall examine in this chapter whether climatic and some natural phenomena occur in cycles, as Earth travels through space in conjunction with other cosmic bodies in a largely cyclic motion. I shall use the research of a radical academic, Dr Raymond H Wheeler, who theorised that major climatic change throughout history has been cyclical, with a major effect on man's behaviour.

Cycles

In my previous book, using the academically accepted chronology, I assumed that the Egyptian Middle Kingdom reached its height c1950 BC. Babylon peaked under Hammurabi c.1750 BC (near the time of the Hyksos invasion of Egypt). The Minoan Middle Kingdom peaked c.1550, in the same era as the Hyksos were expelled. The Egyptian New Kingdom declined from c.1380. The Assyrian

Middle Kingdom lapsed into uncivilised behaviour, even by ancient measures, c.1120 BC, and the New Kingdom peaked c.620. A Phoenician peak c.950 BC (similar to the Hebrew zenith) suggested a possible pattern of recurring peaks of civilisations at two-hundred-year intervals.

When I was earlier researching the theory that ancient oriental philosophy could be combined with modern occidental technology for strategic financial warfare, I discovered many long-cycle theories by scholars. As long ago as 1100 BC, the ancient Etruscans spoke of the Great Year, which they estimated at 1,100 Earth years. They were not far wrong, when their cycle came to an end c.87 BC. Such reckoning would presuppose an end to the civilisation after the Etruscans as c.AD1013AD, which was, in fact, the era when invading Vikings and their Norman descendants dominated southern Italy. The next major civilisation in the Etruscan cycle would be due for termination c.2113.

The German philosopher, Oswald Spengler (*The Decline of the West*, 1918), maintained that there was a definite cycle of cultures that lasted approximately 1,500 years. Spengler theorised that the pattern formed a curved sloping "S" formation (an angled sine curve), in which the early part of the rise was slow (springtime, about five hundred years), the full, often rapid growth (summer and autumn, about eight hundred years), then the last period in which growth was frozen (winter, about four hundred years). Spengler and his American interpreter, Edwin F. Dakin (*Today and Destiny*, c.1940), identified the period AD 1800–2000 as the early part of the winter phase of the current cycle, in which money and democracy would dominate western culture. On their reckoning, the third millennium AD, which has now commenced, should see a rise of "Caesarism" (oligarchic dictatorships) and fading of liberal democracy.

Confucian scholars have been aware of cycles for millennia. From ancient figures, Dr J S Lee, (*The Periodic Recurrence of Internecine Wars in China*, 1931), suggested that two complete and one incomplete eight-hundred-year periods of Chinese history since 221 BC show striking parallelism in their periods of peace and disorder. Towards the end of the cycle, rivalry between North and South would be intensified, causing a change of dynasty from North to South. The next cyclical change is due early in the third millennium, and, if on schedule, political affairs would suggest that Shanghai or the claimed southern province of Taiwan will be involved. Such a major change would need to be triggered by a major crisis, which might well have a financial origin.

Well before Confucius, the Chinese believed that all natural phenomena could be governed by the rhythmic alternation of the fundamental forces of *yin* and *yang*, in which time flows through beneficial and adverse periods that can be represented by the movement of a sine curve.

Ancient Babylonian astrologers recognised similar cyclical patterns over long periods of time, but before I get too far into my theme, let me define *cycles*. A cycle is simply a regularly occurring sequence of similar events. Cycles can be short-, intermediate-, or long-term in length. The sun rising every morning and setting in the evening is a cycle – a very short-term cycle in all our lives. The day represents the rotation of the earth in a cycle of approximately twenty-four hours, which has changed little in millennia. The four seasons, spring, summer, autumn, and winter, are phases of another short-term cycle lasting in totality the solar year of approximately 365 days which the Earth takes to rotate around the sun.

These cycles can be graphically represented also by a sine curve; by combining the daily rotation-cycle curve with the seasonal sine pattern, one can get an illustration of average temperature. One might even forecast a likely temperature for a given time of day on any given date, with the knowledge that other factors would mean that the forecast could only be approximate.

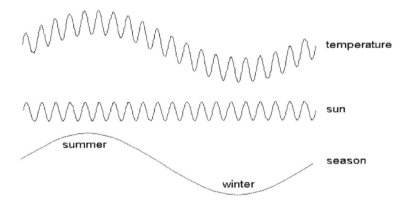

I have included above the sine-wave description of a rhythmic cycle, early in this chapter, to indicate that time flows forwards in a sine wave (lazy "S" wave) and not as a circle, from the Greek root of which the word "cycle" is derived. The cycles I seek to identify are rhythmic cycles which have relatively regular time periods between the troughs and troughs and/or peaks and troughs. The degree of amplitude of peaks and troughs can and does vary in rhythmic cycles, so that with current technology, one cannot identify accurately the exact cyclical turning points, neither in time nor amplitude. However, I hope that I will demonstrate that one can use the cyclical rhythm to make cyclical projections to indicate likely timing of a change of trend, even over centuries.

Daily, annual, and monthly cycles have been observed by human societies for millennia. Herodotus reported that in 341 generations of Egyptian kings/priests, the sun had twice moved from rising in the east to rising in the west and then back again. Ancient priests gained political power from their ability to calculate the times when seasons change, when planting should take place, and when harvesting should occur.

According to ancient Egyptian records, the Earth has had in the past a 360-day solar year. Dr Velikovsky has theorised that the 365.25 solar day year came into being in the eighth century BC, when the Earth's orbit was nudged by Mars. December 25 was respected for millennia as the time when the sun was furthest from Earth, so that various gods were worshipped to ensure the return of the Sun to Earth. Christianity usurped that ancient day for its religion as the birth date of Jesus Christ, who could then be said to be responsible for the return of the sun to Earth.

The ancient Chinese, Hebrews, and Mayans used a lunar cycle in their calendars. There was a 13 lunar-month, 384-day year. In Chinese calculations a complete long-term cycle was 360 years – 90 years hot-dry; 90 years hot-wet; 90 years cold-dry; 90 years cold-wet. I can also note that three complete lunar long-term cycles (3 x 360 x 384 days) equates to 1,136 solar years, close to the Etruscan super-cycle.

In their calendar, the Chinese still use the monthly lunar cycle as the moon rotates around the earth in approximately 29 days. The Western world now uses a more even mathematical monthly model so as to avoid conflict with the solar year. All women in the world are aware that their biological clock operates on a lunar cycle of approximately 29 days, and many societies have relied on forecasts of that cycle to control population numbers.

Fishermen throughout the ages have been aware that the moon produces high and low tides of bodies of water from which they make their living. Modern American scientists have recently discovered that the Moon's effect on Earth is more far-reaching. Major earthquakes and volcanic eruptions have been found to occur at or near the New Moon phase, against statistical odds of such clustering of 1 in 10 million.

If it is logical to assume that the moon, earth and sun can produce cycles which affect humans, then other cosmic bodies might also produce cycles that have a less perceptible effect. Such cosmic cycles are of longer duration than would be noticed by the majority of population, but have been calculated by priests, astrologers and astronomers. Priestly mathematicians in ancient societies could gain much power if their calculated cyclical forecasts proved correct, so it is also logical that long cycles would be kept secret from the general population. It is also rational to assume that later priests, who believed that all matters earthly and cosmic occurred due to the grace of one god, might seek to demean any long secular cyclical theories.

Modern astronomy is overcoming its fear of the fate of Galileo to produce evidence of long cycles. In the third millennium after Christ, the Church and politicians might even admit that secular cycles exist.

Planetary Cycles

Modern man has three cycles on which to base some stability; the daily spin of the planet Earth; the revolution of the Moon around Earth which produces the lunar month; and the revolution of the Earth around the Sun which produces the solar year, and the four seasons. As well as those movements of the Sun, Moon and Earth, most people are aware that the other seven planets in the solar system rotate around the sun at various speeds, even though not much attention is paid to planetary movement by busy modern man. Ancient peoples, without computers and television, were much occupied with the planets from which much of religion was derived.

The planet closest to the Sun is Mercury with a short solar year of 88 earth days. Next from the Sun is Venus, the closest planet to Earth with a year of 224 earth days. Mars with a year of nearly two Earth years (687 days) is Earth's outside companion. The larger more distant planets are Jupiter (solar orbit 11.86 Earth years), Saturn (29.45 years), Uranus (84 years), Neptune (164.45 years) and Pluto (248.5) years.

Two lesser known planets with long elliptical comet-like orbits have been identified in the last few decades - Chiron and Nibiru. Chiron was sighted in 1977 orbiting between Saturn and Uranus around the sun in a revolution of 49-50 years. Astrologers call Chiron a planet, but astronomers have labelled it an asteroid.

Nibiru, sometimes called "Planet X" was known to Sumerian astronomers/ astrologers in the fourth/third millennium BC. Even now, not too much is known of Nibiru which was sighted by IRAS satellite in 1983 with a 3500-3600 year elliptical orbit three times further from the Sun than Pluto. The closest orbital point of Nibiru to the sun, called perihelion, was calculated to be the asteroid belt between Mars and Jupiter last visited c.100BC-0BC. Further information is needed before scientists will theorise about Nibiru, but astrologers suggest that it might have been the bright light in the sky reported at the time of the birth of Christ. Future generations might have to wait another millennium before theories are proven or disproved, that Nibiru was responsible for a collision that produced the asteroid belt, and the disruption to Earth's atmosphere that produced the deluge known as the Great Flood c.3200BC.

The movements of planets have been used for millennia by astrologers to determine future human activity, but the scientific age and a multitude of populist astrologers have caused the general population to pay less heed to these informed mathematicians. Astronomers have started to pay more attention to astrological research and examine some scientific effects of planetary movements on Earth.

Meteorologists in the National Climate Analysis Centre have incorporated the cycle of sunspot intensity into computer algorithms. In the three hundred year long history of documented sunspot activity, peaks in the number of sunspots have been identified every fifth of the average eleven year period - a relative peak every fifty five years. The last major peak commenced in 1976 which suggests c.2031 as another.

In the 1970s, Chinese astronomical research came to light suggesting that the combined magnetic forces of the planets, when in synod (conjunction in a narrow area), could influence the actions of the sun, and cause sunspots and flares which would cause climate change on earth. Labelled the Jupiter Effect, the combined pull of solar planets in the same segment of the heavens as Jupiter (300 times the mass of earth) was calculated to affect Earth 1980-93 in the type of combination that could occur in an approximate cycle of 1000 years.

Changes to the earth's magnetic field were measured during that period, and further calculations suggested that the gravitational effect of Jupiter on solar radiation, was linked to the well-researched eleven year average sunspot cycle, and in conjunction with Saturn, had produced weather effects in a 179 year cycle since 1600AD. The Jupiter/Saturn Effect 179 year cycle was used to predict a San Francisco earthquake in 1982, which did not occur as forecast. However quakes did occur in Los Angeles in 1979, the eruptions of volcanoes Mount St. Helens (Washington 1980) and El Chichon (Mexico 1982). This suggested that a planetary conjunction theory of volcanic and solar activity had some validity.

Climatology is not yet a science, but evidence is growing that climate records can be matched with the historical record of the sun's fluctuations. Chinese scientists have the benefit of 5000 years of climate records, as well as social history and some astronomical data over a similarly long period. Analysis of these records suggests that a number of cold and warm spells coincided with planetary synods. Such research has recently been eclipsed by the political debate over Global Warming because of burning fossil fuel.

Australian and American scientists have used geology to confirm the eleven year sunspot cycle, and the double sunspot cycle of 22 years. There has been a De Vries 200 year solar cycle connected by Russian and Chinese scientists (Rasponov et al) which suggests imminent cooling. A longer 350-314 year cycle has also been identified from 1300 years of sediment deposits. The period 1645-1712, which has been called a Little Ice Age, coincided with an abnormally low number of sunspots, known as a "Maunder Minimum". Some of the more notable effects of the Maunder Minimum included the appearance of glaciers in the Alps advancing farther southward, a frozen North Sea, and the famous year in London without a summer where it remained cold for 21 consecutive months.

An earlier period of low sunspots, the Sporer Minimum of 1400-1510 was also known as a "Little Ice Age." Increased rates of famine in the world were noticed in the Sporer Minimum, and the Baltic Sea froze solid in the winter of 1422-23. If a 300-350 year cycle is relevant, the period 1995-2062 might see Global Warming offset by cooler temperatures from the sunspot cycle.

The link between cyclical solar activity and earth's earthquake and volcanic eruptions is not yet proven to science's satisfaction, but there is no doubt that volcanic eruptions have had a deteriorating effect on the global climate. Scientists have linked famine in China to a 205BC Iceland eruption, and crop failures in Mesopotamia from a New Guinea volcano in 536AD. The average temperature in England dropped 4.5°F in 1815, following the second largest known explosion of Tambora in the Dutch East Indies. Neighbouring volcano Krakatau in 1883 caused a 20 percent reduction in solar radiation in Montpelier, France over three years. Although not yet related to the cosmos, a 180 year earth stress cycle, 100 year and a lesser seven year volcanic cycles have been identified by the University of East Anglia.

In addition to movements of the planets, there are comets which regularly visit Earth. Most famous of these comets is Halley's Comet which was discovered in 1705 after Edmond Halley had computed parabolic orbits for 24 comets observed from 1337 to 1698. His analysis of the list revealed the comets of 1531, 1607, and 1682 moved in almost identical orbits and were separated by intervals of roughly 75 years. Ultimately, 23 previous appearances were identified, indicating that the comet had been seen at every return going back to the year 240BC. In that year the Chinese observed a "broom star" that *appeared in the east and then was seen in the north.* The comet and Earth experienced their closest approach to one another on April 10, 837 when their separating distance equalled 0.0342 AU (3.2 million miles).

A contemporary of Edmond Halley, William Whiston, published in 1696 his New Theory of the Earth in which he claimed a comet of a 575.5 year periodicity. Whiston, then a fellow of Cambridge University, had become a devoted pupil of Newton in 1694, seven years after the first edition of the *Principia*. Whiston's comet had appeared in 1682, 1106, 531, and in September of 44BC. Whiston further asserted that this comet had met the earth in 2346BC, and caused the Deluge.

Whiston found references in classical literature to the change in inclination of the terrestrial axis and, ascribing it to a displacement of the poles by his comet, concluded that before the Deluge the planes of daily rotation and yearly revolution coincided. He also found references to a year consisting of 360 days only, although the Greek authors referred the change to the time of Atreus and Thyestes, and the Romans to the time of Numa, c.700BC. In the East a new calendar of 365 days was apparently introduced by the Babylonian Nabonassar (in 747BC). Whiston however ascribed these changes to the effect of the Earth's encounter with the comet of the Deluge.

It was suggested early in the twentieth century that the 531AD (actually 530) comet was in fact an early apparition of Halley's 75-year-period comet. It was also suspected that the 1106 comet was a member of the close Sun-orbiting comet group. Wriston's theories might have been countered but one needs to wait until later this millennium to be sure.

Cyclical Behaviour

There is an abundance of reading available on cycles which can convince even the most sceptical that human nature is affected by cyclical effects. In 1940

Edward R. Dewey formed the Foundation for the Study of Cycles which was then affiliated with the University of Pittsburgh, Pennsylvania. The Foundation has recorded thousands of cycles, from a 9.6 year animal breeding cycle to a 142 year cycle in international battles. Since this book is concerned with the evolution of war-like capitalism, it is worth mentioning that Edward Dewey identified war cycles of duration 57 years, 21.98 years (116 repetitions of a cycle over a period of 2500 years), 17.71years and 11.24 years.

One combination of cycles allowed Dewey to predict in 1952 that minor wars would escalate in the 1960's with the possibility of a combat double peak at the beginning and the end of the decade. History recorded a peak in the 1950/1960's (India-China, Holland-Indonesia, Syria-Egypt, Tibet-China) followed by the concentrated international conflict in the 1960/1970's in Vietnam.

As long ago as 2256BC the Chinese organised their calendar in a sixty year cycle. The so-called Aubrey holes at Stonehenge in England have suggested that sometime between 1600 and 2000BC, the builders of the celestial clock used a fifty six year cycle. The classic South American Mayas regularly worked with a fifty two year cycle.

What if I return to a cyclical analogy with the weather? The most regular weather cycle which we experience each year of our lives is the seasonal cycle. Edward Dewey uses the seasonal cycle as the metaphor for a long term economic wave.

"In the beginning of the wave's upward sweep, the economy is just ending a time of depression, when as in winter few things grew. Storms have stripped down the decaying trees and weak limbs that could not stand the testing of tempests. People begin to sense in the air a kind of burgeoning opportunity, like a faint smell of spring when there is no change yet visible to the eye.

Venture capital starts coming forth - when industries that got started in a small way toward the autumn of the last cycle now begin to find growing opportunities - when even the most casual scatterings of seed may spring up into a lush growth. The great industrial innovations that rise in such a springtime were usually planted in the previous cycle.

A multifarious number of other contributory industries rise simultaneously, some great, some small; and as they thrive, so do older industries. Employment grows; money starts flowing; credit expands. When midsummer has arrived, when the peak of the growing cycle is reached, there seem a million evidences around of a new era, a florid age of growth beyond the memory of living man. Speculation regarding the boundless future is rife.

But now the summer storm gathers; suddenly from nowhere clouds appear, the barometer suddenly falls, and in the quick hail and rains and winds, there is much scurrying in from the fields. When the sun comes out again, the humidity is drained from the air, and in its clear light there is already a hint of autumn.

This late summer and coming autumn is the period of great harvest - when the products of industry usually are distributed more widely than ever before. Prices have come down from their peak. And, although they will form occasional tables (plateaus), they now usually continue to drift generally downward - while wages on the whole stay up. This means growing purchasing power for the workers who have jobs. It makes a special kind of proletarian prosperity, where the benefits of the economy are now even more widely shared than in the days when industrial expansion was so rapid.

There is unfortunately more unemployment. For as prices decline, manufacturers naturally look for ways to eliminate extra man-hours, to turn out their product for less. And competition grows among the manufacturers. Newcomers spring up, attracted by the records of lush profits made by those long in the field.

People begin to try to hold onto what they have. Some of the old enterprise has lost its fervor. There are bursts of speculations now and then, but the great progress of the era has now been made. As it slowly draws to an end, people look backward to the past midsummer days when great fortunes could sometimes be found almost by turning over a stone if you were lucky; and jobs were everywhere; and unprecedental industrial and economic achievements were transforming the landscape. And the people begin to wonder if progress has really stopped".

I have not paraphrased Dewey's words; firstly because I could not have explained the economic seasonal cycle any better; and secondly to reproduce sixty years later, the feeling of the 1940s. I can discern a smell of economic autumn in 2014.

In more modern research, a New Zealand economist, Ray Tomes, produced a Harmonic Theory which developed harmonics of a 35.6year cycle that coincided with earlier cyclical research. Harmonics of 35.6years produce such smaller cycles as 3.96 years (similar to the Business Cycle), 11.87 years (similar to the sun-spot cycle) and 17.8 years (similar to a real estate cycle). Larger cycles are also harmonics - 108 years (similar to the climatic/political cycle) 54years (similar to the Kondratieff cycle) and 36years (similar to New Zealand economy). 178years multiplied by 13 is 2315 years which is very close to a large climatic cycle of 2300years.

Climatic Cycles

A number of studies have confirmed the theory of a 35 year European weather cycle, mentioned by Sir Francis Bacon in the sixteenth century and later published by E. Bruckner in Austria 1891. A 22 year weather pattern has also been identified, which has caused a great deal of interest in recent years, because of some correlation with a double 11 year cycle of sun spot activity. I have mentioned the link between solar activity and volcanic eruptions which spew dust into the upper atmosphere with a tendency to cool the earth's climate. The atmospheric dust from volcanoes alone makes it imperative that the long term cyclical weather patterns should not be ignored, even when the cause of the cycles might be not apparent.

Dr Raymond H. Wheeler of the Psychology Department at the University of Kansas developed a theory on the effect of cyclical changes in climate on society and civilisation, without trying to examine the likely causes for such cycles. Wheeler's studies appeared in a controversial book *"Climate - The Key to Understanding Business Cycles"* (by Raymond H. Wheeler; Edited by Michael Zahorchak; Tide Press; Linden, New Jersey 1991). Wheeler began his research in the 1930s while teaching at the University of Kansas, and over the next twenty years with over 200 research associates surveyed 18 areas of human activity in relation to climatic fluctuations 600BC-1950AD.

Many of Dr Wheeler's papers were unpublished on his death, and the late Michael Zahorchak undertook to extend the research and publish. It is a pity that Dr Wheeler's theories have not been more publicised, although I suspect that, like Velikovsky, some theories were outside the mainstream thought of his time, and would have attracted academic animosity of specialists outside his own field of psychology. In *"Life/Death Rhythms of Ancient Empires"* I utilised some extensions of Dr Wheeler's long term cyclical theories for the period 3200BC-1400AD. In this book I shall examine Dr Wheeler's long and short term cyclical theories for the period 1400AD-2020AD which, together with economic cycles, that I have utilised successfully in twentieth century financial risk management.

Wheeler and his team used lake levels, tree rings and sunspots to gather evidence of climatic trends. He utilised much of the work on climate published by Professor Ellsworth Huntington who had examined the Mediterranean, Caspian Sea, European and American lakes. Other lake level data was studied from the Caucasus, Palestine, central Asia, Australia and South America. River levels were also studied, including seasonal floods of the Nile. The sequoia tree-ring studies of Douglass, Huntington and Antevs were used to indicate the trees' growing climate. Where possible, other trees from different areas were studied to confirm the findings from the sequoias. I understand that Wheeler's data in now held in New York at the Market Technicians Association offices. Wheeler's studies of history and climatic fluctuations over the period 600 BC to 1950 AD revealed distinct cyclical climatic phases --- warm-wet, warm-dry, cold-wet, cold-dry.

Wheeler suggested that prior to 575BC cycles were irregular without suggesting cause, but which would be in accord with the planet Earth settling into a new orbit after disturbances suggested by Velikovsky. After 575BC 1000 year cycles have been identified in which cold-dry maxima as occurring at around 575BC, 460AD, and 1475. Even though there are variations of intensity in these climatic peaks and troughs, we can look at notable changes to societies around theses periods. 500 year cycles have been identified in which climate was dry and colder than normal centred on 30AD, 955AD, and possibly 1975AD. After 955, the 1000s were so warm that trees grew in Iceland. The phases of most interest in this book are the 100 year cycles, cold-dry troughs of which have been identified as 1400, 1475, 1570, 1655, 1765, 1865 and 1960?. After 1300, winters became longer and the summer growing season grew shorter. There was little relief from the cold cyclical peaks until 1870. In Northern Europe the period was called the Little Ice Age.

Professor Mike Baillie, an authority on dendrochronology and palaeoecology at Queen's University, Belfast, has presented a fascinating scientific detective story independently after Wheeler's death. The story starts with the description of decades long collaborative effort by many scientists to develop a worldwide record of climate modulated, annual tree growth as recorded in tree growth rings (dendrochronology). The five harshest environmental events showing in the dendrochronology records are events at 2354-2345 BC, 1628-1623 BC, 1159-1141 BC, 208-204 BC, and 536-545 AD. In terms of climate, these time periods appear similar in that the growth ring evidence implies colder than usual temperatures and unusual rainfall patterns.

I note that 1628BC was the carbon-dated period for the great volcanic explosion of the Minoan island of Thera (Santorini). Professor Baillie has expounded his theory that, around AD 540, the earth may have had a close encounter with a comet, plunging the planet into several 'years without a summer', spreading famine across its surface, and spawning a host of myths by which traumatised people tried to explain and control a disintegrating world. Such a time would be coincident with Whiston's comet.

The Climate and Society

As long ago as the Classical Age in Greece, philosophers noted that peoples living in the cooler, northern regions were lighter coloured and stronger than those who resided in warmer southern climates. The northern barbarians were more vigorous, braver, more aggressive and ferocious in battle, and less prone to sensuous indulgence. Their societies were more likely to follow elected leaders, and did not practice slavery. On the other hand, peoples from the warmer regions of the Mediterranean were darker skinned, more sensitive, more intelligent, more disciplined in battle, hot tempered, passionate and prone to sexual indulgence. Southern civilisations tended towards tyrannical rule, more given to intrigue and assassinations, inclined to slavery and in general more cruel.

Aristotle (384-322BC) wrote that the northern European had more spirit and vigour than the native of the warm Asiatic regions, who was content to remain in subjection and slavery. He believed that an intermediate climate between the cold of Europe and the warmth of Asia produced superior people. Vitruvius, a Roman contemporary of Strabo (c.63BC-c.21AD), concluded that people from northern climes were larger, more vigorous, braver in battle and had deeper voices than people of the south who were smaller, more timid, darker and had higher pitched voices.

Vitruvius also believed that the greater intelligence of southern races was due in part to the fact that warmth was conducive to greater reflection. Byzantine Emperor Julian (*the Apostate* 331-363AD) adversely contrasted the industrious Gauls against the effeminate Syrians.

Twelfth century Arab geographers reached the same conclusions as their ancient predecessors, but also noted that the temperament and behaviour patterns of races that migrated from one climate to another changed, until they resembled the characteristics of those which prevailed in the new climate.

In the *Age of Reason*, the French philosopher who influenced the American Constitution, C.L. Montesquieu (1689-1755), found that warm climate races were weak, timid, apathetic to physical exertion, avaricious, sensitive to pleasure and pain, sexually indulgent, and exhibited little "mental ambition". They were also more religious, stubborn and wilful; their codes of law were stricter and their governments more tyrannical. The inhabitants of the north (of whom admittedly, Montesquieu was one) were found to be more democratic, more apt to be honest, emotionally more stable, and less prone to expending their energies in sensuous pleasures. Such public observations would be impossible to broadcast in today's *Age of Political Correctness*, whether true or not.

It was not until the 20th century that philosophers and geographers made a connection between the influences of climate on man's behaviour. J. Russell Smith (*Industrial and Commercial Geography* 1913) believed that cool temperatures were a great stimulus to human activity and affected nations as well as individuals. Civilisation, he wrote, is the product of adversity and thrives best where man must work hard or starve. Therefore, to an extent little appreciated, environment makes the race. Racial characteristics are not inborn but are determined by the environment, or at least were initially so determined.

An American economist, Henry L. Moore (*Economic Cycles, Their Law and Cause* 1914) wrote that an alternation of buoyant and depressed attitudes seems to be environmentally conditioned, and that economic cycles follow cycles in crop yields, which in turn depend on rainfall cycles.

It was the conclusion of a Russian, Tchijewski, in the 1930s that increased electrical activity in the sun, especially around sunspot maxima, increased ionization of the air. He believed this in turn stimulated mankind both physiologically and psychologically, with effects that could be traced throughout all social relationships.

Professor of Experimental Medicine at the Cincinnati Medical School, Dr Clarence A. Mills, conducted studies on disease/death rates of people from various racial and regional origins. He found that persons dying from tuberculosis who came from USA Gulf states succumbed to the disease in half the time of people raised in the North. White immigrants from warmer, southern countries of Europe lived only 11 months with the disease, compared to 21 months for northern Europeans. Black people born and raised in the South resisted the disease for only 9 months, while those from the North survived 17 months.

The death rate from acute appendicitis in various regions increased as the studies moved from north to south. During the 1920s and 1930s the world experienced relatively high temperatures, which in the USA broke previous records. Dr Mills found that around 1930 stature had commenced to decline, girls were slower in menstruating and 20 year-old boys were on average less mature.

He contrasted this assessment with the long cold periods between 1830 and 1900, which produced young men of mature personalities and rugged bodies.

Yale Professor Ellsworth Huntington (1876-1947) was an economic geographer who published 28 books on civilisation, environment, racial differences and climate. He claimed that southeast England had the best climate in the world for human health, stability and advancement. He suggested that there should be cool but not excessively cold winters for mental stimulation, and comfortably warm but not hot summers for physical stimulation. Huntington was convinced that climatic variations were world wide, although their precise form differed from place to place. Well before the term Global Warming was coined, he noted that there is an almost uniform decrease in rainfall along the equator at times of increased solar activity. It was Huntington who observed that periods of prosperity and decline of the Roman Empire corresponded with growth maxima and minima of the Californian sequoias, although he used the term climatic pulses rather than cycles.

In the 1960s the presence of a biological clock in living things was confirmed, and the daily rhythm that a body's biology followed was designated a circadian clock. The biological clock was shown to be affected by temperature, and the circadian clock in some plants and animals actually stopped when the temperature fell below a threshold around freezing.

Dr Raymond Wheeler went far back in history to 600 BC and postulated that over 90% of the world's great leaders and almost 70% of its most enlightened leaders have governed from a cold to warm climate and the subsequent warm wet phases. 96% of those rulers regarded by historians as being poor rulers have governed during the warm dry and cold periods of history. Wheeler's theories suggested that we should not have expected great leaders in the 1990s.

Wheeler's studies raised evidence that climatic fluctuations repeat themselves in a definite succession. As it turns warm after a cold period, the weather is at first very wet, but eventually turns dry. The heat climax comes during the drought. Then as it turns cold, rainfall picks up. Before it turns warm again there occurs another series of droughts during which the cold climax is reached. In historic time, the transition from cold to warm periods has been attended by cultural revivals and eras of prosperity. For centuries, migrations reached a climax during the cold and dry phase of the climatic cycle, and great civilisations declined.

Dr Wheeler postulated that during cold-dry phases of the climatic cycle, which were often long and drawn out, civilisation was depressed and at times disintegrated. Chaos, anarchy and piracy prevailed. The world writhed with migrations. Having lived through the testing cold-dry phase, peoples are chastened, invigorated and hardened.

Then, in the springtime of the climatic cycle, social, economic and political forces become better organised and unified. Often influenced by strong individuals, governments focus their power and efficiency, to enjoy the prosperity and vitality of the warm-wet period.

As warmth increases and moisture declines, populations tend to become complacent. Vitality ebbs and prosperity fades. The aristocracy becomes reactionary and despotic, so that civilisations became decadent in hot dry phases. In economic terms hot-dry periods have experienced economic stagnation and depression. As tyrannical government is unable to be maintained, insurrections occur.

As the weather cools and moisture increases, leadership flows to the lower classes and younger generation which however lack experience and calibre. Governments then gain experience to be able to recreate wealth so that Wheeler suggests society is more civilised and democratic in cold-wet phases, which is the second-best time in history. Democracy then grows to become unwieldy with too many voices in government, and strong individuals attract wealth disproportionately which tends to reduce the middle class. Civilisation declines into the cold-dry phase.

The hot-dry phase has been characterised by dictators, statism, socialism, communism; and cultural, moral and economic decline. Behaviour patterns are introverted. In art, surrealistic and impressionistic patterns develop, and in business, aggressiveness and self confidence decline with subsequent depressions and the collapse of economic systems. Wars often reflected the culmination of the decadence of the previous warm-wet period and became the cruellest type of struggle, with entire populations slaughtered or enslaved. However, as the temperature fell and rainfall increased, activity also increased, crops were again good, and general revival began. The 1930's were an acute example of the hot-dry phase in the USA.

During the cold-dry phase all the evidence pointed to economic depression, or at least recurring recessions. The early 1890's experienced an extended cold-dry period world wide.

Theories, that changing behaviour of societies can be related to climatic change which is cyclical, are at the least considered controversial. The studies that might be needed to provide modern scientific evidence to back-up the theories are unlikely to be undertaken in today's world of *political correctness*. It would be anathema, which might be taken as government inaction, to have studies that would have to find groups of people biologically inferior to other groups of people, or disadvantaged by the climate.

The presence of climatic cycles would suggest that historic societal activity was not in the control of governments, with the corollary that future events might also be out of government control. Even if governments or powerful academic and scientific bodies would fund studies of climatic cycles and human behaviour, it is unlikely that the results would be published in a form that could be understood by the layman. Cyclic studies by the advertising industry are not made public lest the public reacts.

Maybe such studies have already occurred but have been classified top-secret because of strategic implications. I do not expect too much public agreement with the conclusions of this book from many scientists or economists, because the degree of proof is likely to be claimed insufficient. Business men need to be more open-minded.

Economic Cycles

A cyclic economic long wave was first recognised by economists 200 years ago. Long economic cycles of 50-60 years duration were suggested from around 1810 by various economists - Hyde-Clarke, Helphand, de Wolff, Van Geldren and Lord Beveridge. The Russian, Nikolai D. Kondratieff, produced in 1924 the best known systematic attempt to confirm the existence of long waves of economic growth and their inter-relationship with political and social developments, war and revolution. In 1926 he published his results in the German *"Archiv fur Sozialwissenshaft"*.

Kondratieff's study suggested that the beginning of the cycle was a period of new technology and high investment. The expansion of investment causes prices to rise. The increased volume of goods requires a higher velocity of money, causing higher prices, inflation, increased consumption and employment. After about 25 years the expansion reaches a peak; inefficiencies develop; work attitudes change; money is diverted from capital to consumption; prices rise; profits fall; debt increases.

The downswing is brought about by the above inefficiencies which become accentuated during the fall, as wealth consumption expands beyond its limits and debts become harder to service. At lower levels the economy experiences recession/depression which brings about falls in interest rates, wages, material prices and employment around 55 years from the beginning of the cycle. The search for new inventions and manufacturing efficiency then provides the source for the next cyclical upswing.

Harvard Professor Joseph Schumpeter incorporated Kondratieff's theories in his book *"Business Cycles"* (McGraw-Hill Books; 1939). In his time, Schumpeter's cyclical views were overshadowed by John Maynard Keynes whose major work *"The General Theory of Employment, Interest and Money"* appeared in 1936. During the first 18 months in print, Schumpeter's book sold only 1,075 copies. The world had turned to Keynes' fiscal stabilisation methods. Keynes did not address long cycles, possibly because, as he said, *"In the long run we are all dead"*.

Schumpeter differentiated between invention and innovation. He starts at an equilibrium point from which the innovative actions of a few entrepreneurs are copied by many agents to stimulate the business cycle upswing. His peak is exacerbated by an exhaustion of innovation. Schumpeter was fascinated with the role of the entrepreneur whom he believed was primarily responsible for each revival after a recession.

Another base of modern economic theory was that of Karl Marx, whose famous 1867 *"Das Kapital"* criticised the decennial cycle of stagnation, prosperity, overproduction and crisis. More modern economists, Forrester (1976), Mensch (1979), Mandel (1980) and Freeman (1984), have since produced theories from Schumpeter's opinions. Schumpeter suggested the eventual failure of capitalism, but for different reasons to those of Karl Marx. *"The State and Business would expand to such a stage that the entrepreneur would be eliminated, at which time capitalist cycle could not be renewed"*.

A specific modification of the theory of Kondratieff cycles was developed by Daniel Šmihula.

For the era of the modern society and capitalistic economy he defined six long economic waves (cycles) and each of them was initiated by a specific technological revolution:

- 1. (1600–1780) The wave of the Financial-agricultural revolution
- 2. (1780–1880) The wave of the Industrial revolution
- 3. (1880–1940) The wave of the Technical revolution
- 4. (1940–1985) The wave of the scientific-technical revolution

- 5. (1985–2015) The wave of the Information and telecommunications revolution
- 6. (2015-2035?) The hypothetical wave of the post-informational technological revolution

The first international credit crisis occurred in 1557 when Spain defaulted on loans which in turn caused a collapse of other international loans on the Antwerp bourse. Another crisis occurred in 1637 when a wave of speculation on Dutch exchanges over tulip bulbs burst into a sharp collapse. John Law's Mississippi Bubble burst in France in 1719, closely followed by the English South Sea Bubble in 1720. The first modern financial crisis occurred in 1825 after a bubble of South American debt turned sour. The US crash of 1929 continued the sequence of crashes roughly 100 years apart. The crash of 2008 is relatively early in this sequence, but given the rapid expansion of US debt in the late twentieth century, it is quite possible that the economic collapse of the twenty-first century has commenced.

As a grizzled financial warrior, I have not been able to make all decisions in financial and commodities markets based on incontrovertible evidence, because even if it was available, it would have been secret to a select few. Data underlying markets has been available in an untimely and inefficient manner, with a strong bias on production (government) figures, and including insufficient material on consumption. Operators in deregulated markets do not have the luxury of waiting for complete evidence before acting. Market technical analysts, such as myself, have tended to tabulate available figures and theories to reach an educated conclusion on which to act, all the time being aware that the action might have to be reversed as more evidence comes to light.

I can only hope that my interpretation of history and estimated climatic cycles in this book will be considered by the reader as a credible conclusion.

CHAPTER 2

The Ancient/Medieval Cyclic Climatic Social Pattern 3000BC - 1400AD

This book is the sequel to **"Life/Death Rhythms of Ancient/Medieval Empires – Climatic Cycles Influence Rule"** which discussed the cycles of dominant cultures 3000BC – 1400AD. The research from this book is presented below as a summary to form the basis of the cyclical flow of dominant cultures in the capitalist era 1400-2100AD. I am aware as always that many academic historians will not totally agree with the conclusions below. Most historians of my acquaintance do not concentrate on the "big picture", preferring to build reputations of well researched minutiae of history. In my search for a cyclical pattern that transcends time, I must of course distil history down to workable sections.

Cultural Evolution

I define a human "culture" as being a natural way of life in which activities, distinctive to a particular society, are unconsciously accepted by the people in that society as normal behaviour. When a baby learns to speak the language spoken as the mother tongue in the home, the young child will also adopt the mannerisms of the adults observed as role models - the family culture. Groups of children, particularly in the primitive world, adopt the language and natural customs of tribal clans of adults from whom they learn the manners and trade of their society. If the tribe stays isolated, the manners and customs of its society will tend to remain in a static culture, or at least with only slow generational change from the odd internal innovation. An example of an isolated culture is that of the

Australian aborigines, which developed over millennia subject to little contact with any other culture until maybe the seventeenth century *Anno Domini* (AD).

If a tribal group meets another tribal group with different manners and customs, some of the intruders' more efficient or attractive customs will be absorbed by the old culture. The new customs might be peripheral to the old tribal society, in which case the original culture would be little changed. If the new customs were from a dominant tribe, particularly in the case of weapons, the original culture would develop markedly, and many of the old ways might be forgotten. The natives of ancient Mesopotamia, at the crossroads of early trade and migration, are an illustration of a culture that was continually fertilised by ideas of others.

Human cultures developed according to the environment, command and enlightenment that were peculiar to one society made up of groups of tribes, until a change of conditions, including social intercourse with another culture, caused further evolution of the original tribal culture. The most identifiable factor in a culture was religion which in ancient societies tended to be integrated with the rule of the kings. In the ancient world, the culture which achieved dominance, often through military means, extended its cultural influences to the subordinate cultures.

The warrior chief/priest/king from the dawn of time has evolved to become the government/corporate president/chairman of today, governing hierarchical organisations similar in structure to tribes, city/states and empires of the past; employing generals and armies, priests of propaganda, to achieve domination over competitors. By understanding the evolution of human culture through millennia, one can understand the actions of the multi-national corporations which guide so much of our lives in the third Christian millennium.

Innovation, external or internal could have an immediate affect on a culture, but often cultural changes took many decades. I will demonstrate that cultural change has occurred in identifiable cycles of hundreds of year's duration which are still relevant today.

Golden Age Cultures' Common Features

I should once again state my aim of finding a pattern throughout the evolution of mankind that can be of benefit in the future. In my Ancient studies, it was too early in human history to discuss an actual financial capitalist system, even if some of the seeds had already been sown. Elements of the ancient/medieval societies might be classified within the definition of capitalism, but, with the possible exception of the Phoenicians and Venetians, there is insufficient evidence to state that the cultures themselves practised organised capitalism.

As the benchmark of cultural success, I have sought the existence of a just and prosperous society that endured for longer than the life-span of one or two great rulers. I define this society as one which utilizes the resources of its citizens to produce a comfortable way of life with suitable public infrastructure for the majority, as well as to husband surpluses and safeguard reserves to provide relief in times of change.

I have formulated six factors which need to be present for my benchmark of dominant cultural success:-

1. Climate and geographic access to sustainable resources.
2. A strong leadership structure with just sharing of society's surplus that encourages involvement in peaceful advances, as well as defence/war.
3. A cohesive religion that is tolerant of secular innovation
4. Use of technology to produce and protect prosperity.
5. Codified broadcast laws, capable of being enforced to ensure order.
6. The ability to safeguard civil and cultural integrity in war and peace.

The best of these cultures have given historians the "golden ages" when civilisation thrived.

If Dr. Raymond Wheeler's hypothesis held true that "golden ages" throughout history have occurred within every second 100 year climatic cycle, then a pattern should be able to be identified in the dominant cultures that I have just outlined. Of course, I am aware that patterns, like beauty, are often in the eye of the beholder, rather than being immediately self-evident. I do not expect all academic historians to agree with my opinions, and it will be up to the readers to decide whether the patterns that I identify are similarly perceptible to their eye.

Timing Patterns

Two possible golden periods could possibly be identified in Egyptian culture

- the Twelfth Dynasty Middle Kingdom 1990 – 1790BC,
- the Eighteenth Dynasty New Kingdom 1520 – 1325BC

The dominance of the Phoenician golden culture commenced c.1075BC, peaked c.950 - 900BC and had faded c.700BC.

The military Assyrian culture did not find my favour as a just, enduring, prosperous society, however there could have been a golden period in Assyrian terms 860 – 640BC.

The supremacy of the Achaemenid Persians commenced c.550BC, peaked c.510BC and had faded c.360BC. There was relative peace but only limited increases in human endeavours.

The classic Greek culture failed to present as a just, enduring, prosperous society, despite providing the cultural seeds for the later growth of great civilisations. A possible golden age could be identified somewhat consistent with the Persian period from c.546 - c.338BC

The Carthaginian culture also failed my benchmarks but, on the little that is known, possibly enjoyed a golden age c.450 - 250BC.

The Hellenisation of the Mediterranean and bordering areas of Asia was led by Ptolemaic Egypt which quickly gained dominance c.300BC, peaked c.246BC, and had reached insignificance by 100BC.

The Roman Republic became a prosperous force to be reckoned with c.275BC, peaked 167BC but any golden age was lost to Roman Empire culture c.80BC.

The Roman Empire could not be considered a just, prosperous society, even though there is no doubt that its control of huge areas of the world, endured with some prosperity. The early period could be classified as golden 20BC – 190AD.

The decline of the Roman Empire and the Parthians allowed the Persian Sassanid Empire to flourish and its golden period could be counted as 325-575AD.

The Roman imperial world was superseded by the dominant culture of the Catholic Church, but the era was that of insurrection and could not be considered prosperous. Human endeavours were stifled by Church dogma until the later flowering of the Renaissance.

China suffered from large periods of warfare and in periods of relative peace could produce only limited increases in human endeavours. Two possible golden ages were under the Western Han 210BC-2AD and the successor Eastern Han dynasty 25-220AD.

India enjoyed a golden periods in the Mauryan Empire 322-185BC and in the Gupta Empire 300-470AD.

Golden ages for different cultures were few and far between in the medieval period because of the difficult melding of cultures into evolving civilisations. In the main, golden ages were the product of a single ruler that occasionally lasted into the next generation.

The Chinese T'ang dynasty enjoyed a golden age c.630-690. The Muslim golden age could be said to be 660-800 under the Umayyad and Abbasid dynasties. Some non-Catholic historians have identified 770-850 in Umayyad Spain as a golden age. The Carolingian golden age only lasted 737-814. An Indian golden age occurred under the Cholas 985-1040. China enjoyed a golden age under the Northern Sung 960-1126 and possibly under the Southern Sung 1195-1225.

Ancient Chronology

	Culture	Peak	Peak Climate	Overall Period
1990–1790BC	Egyptian Middle	1926BC		200 year period
1520–1325BC	Egyptian New	1385BC		195 year period
1075–700BC	Phoenician	900BC		375 year period
860–640BC	Assyrian	700BC		220 year period
550–360BC	Achaemenid	510BC	cold-dry	190 year period
545–340BC	Classic Greek	505BC	cold-dry	205 year period
450–250BC	Carthaginian	300BC	cold-dry	200 year period
320–185BC	India Maurya	280BC	cold-dry	135 year period
300–100BC	Hellenistic	246BC	cold-dry	200 year period
275–80BC	Roman Republic	167BC	cold-dry	195 year period
210BC–2AD	China Western Han	90BC	cold-dry	212 year period
20BC–190AD	Roman Empire	160AD	hot-dry	210 year period
25–220AD	China Eastern Han	125AD	cold-dry	195 year period
325–622AD	Sassanid Persian	575AD	cold-dry	297 year period
300–470AD	India Gupta Empire	380AD	warm-wet	170 year period

Medieval Chronology

	Culture	Peak	Pk Climate	Peak Period	Overall Period
361-700AD	Byzantine Empire	630	cold/wet	269yrs	339yrs
581-900	Chinese Sui and T'ang	690	hot/dry	109yrs	319yrs
560-900	Indian Pallava	780	warm/wet	220yrs	340yrs
632-970	Arab Muslim	809	hot/dry	177yrs	338yrs
650-868	Holy Roman Frank	814	hot/dry	164yrs	218yrs
900-1215	Tamil Hindu Chola	1040	warm/wet	140yrs	315yrs
911-1220	Catholic Norman	1170	cold/dry	259yrs	309yrs
919-1250	Holy Roman German	1077	warm/wet	158yrs	331yrs
960-1276	Chinese Sung dynasty	1127	cold/dry	167yrs	303yrs
1073-1378	Holy Roman Empire	1216	warm/wet	143yrs	305yrs
1172-1473	Venice	1348	cold	225yrs	350yrs
1206-1395	Mongol	1274	cold/wet	68yrs	189yrs

The periods of ancient golden cultural dominance vary from 375 years to 195 years in the West, and 170 to 135 years in India, which might be explained by the geographic area controlled directly by each culture. The times which I have roughly identified as times of peak cultural influence can be placed within the pattern of time periods according to Dr. Wheeler's hypothesis.

The periods of medieval cultural dominance vary from 339 years to 218 years in the West and 338 to 189 years in the Orient, which is similar enough despite the geographic area controlled directly by each culture. The periods of dominance appear to have increased from rough average 200 year of ancient times to around 300 medieval years. Similarly the start-to-peak times have increased to 68-269yrs.

A secondary theory can be suggested that pervasive elements of dominant cultures persist for around 1000 years. I have noted that the period of Amun-Re as dominant Egyptian god lasted for the Middle and New Kingdoms 1990 – 1070, a period of 900 years.

The Phoenician/Carthaginian commercial culture extended 1000 years 1100 -100BC.

The Greco-Roman culture apparently lasted 975 years from Solon c.590BC until the death of Justinian in 565AD.

The Byzantine culture could be said to have influenced Asia-Minor, Eastern Europe to the European Renaissance 476-1453AD.

Western Asia could be said to have been influenced by the Persians for over a 1000 years. If the Achaemenid, Parthian and Sassanid Empires could be combined in time, the total period would have been 1125 years.

The concept of a Holy Roman Empire in Europe could be said to have extended between 650 to the end of the Catholic Counter Reformation in 1648.

The military advances of Islam could be said to have lasted from 632 under Mohammed until 1686 when the Holy League liberated Buda from the Ottoman Empire.

Patterns of Geographic Access to Resources

The Phoenicians were pressured, possibly from increasing population and lack of land resources in Canaan, to develop access to resources by land and sea over a wide-ranging geographic area. Colonies were planted to protect access to resources.

The Achaemenid's also commenced with meagre resources in their homelands of Media and Persia, but through military conquest expanded throughout most of the then known world to create almost limitless wealth. The colonisation of conquered nations was tolerant through the offices of *satraps*, in control of military forces of the regions. Through the *satraps*, the emperor could command every necessary resource.

Egypt had a long history as a fertile grain bowl, and occasional occupations of Asian areas. It had then been neglected as a *satrapy* by the later Achaemenid Persians. The colonisation of Egypt by the Macedonians and Greeks expanded Egyptian agricultural production through the use of imported Hellenistic techniques. The wealth gained from grain exports financed access to those Mediterranean resources which were not freely available within Egypt.

Much of the land surrounding the early city of Rome was barely fertile, particularly as forests were cleared, so population growth forced the Romans to colonise agricultural areas belonging to other peoples on the Italian peninsular. It was natural that contact internationally through wars against the Macedonians and

Carthaginians, would lead the Romans then to colonise Europe and throughout the Mediterranean to gain access to the resources that Italy lacked.

The Empires of both India and China became more prosperous when they could control the southern states of their regions. The Mauryan economy was driven by agriculture. The State owned huge farms and these were cultivated by slaves and farm laborers. Taxes collected on land, trade and manufacture of handicrafts were the other major sources of income during this era.

The Byzantines had access to Greece, the Balkans and the close Middle East. Even though they were in conflict with the surrounding cultures, they had more than enough resources to keep the shrunken Empire alive. In addition, because of the geographic position of Constantinople (Byzantium), trade routes converged on Empire to provide taxes to keep the administration and military active. In the later period, the Empire became starved of resources as hostile forces encroached on its territory.

The Arab Muslims controlled the Middle East, North Coast of Africa, some of Italy and most of Spain during their period in power. Although the Arabs lost power to new Muslim leaders, the area under control did not vary much. The Mediterranean became a Muslim pond so they were able to dominate maritime trade.

The Frank Catholics had control of the major part of what became modern Europe. Although the region was still developing agriculturally there was more than enough produce to encourage peaceful prosperity during the breaks between wars.

The Indian Chola Empire dominated the south of India and included territories in Ceylon (Sri Lanka). Its influence and trade went as far east as Cambodia, south to Java and west to the Maldives.

The expansion from Scandinavian raiders to Norman rulers extended Norse culture.

The Catholic Norman Empire comprised England and much of France. At its height under Henry II the territory stretched from the Scottish border to the march of Spain with the notable exception of Ile de France and a few associated counties. The lesser Normans dominated the south of Italy, Sicily and the Holy Land. The Norsemen were the founders of the Rus in a fertile area of Russia.

The Holy Roman Empire dominated Germany and the Italian north. The popes' influence during this period extended throughout Europe and the Holy Land. A great portion of the Church tithes went to Rome.

Venice was not a great coloniser until late in empire, but it controlled the trade routes to allow economic dominance of Europe. Its control of strategic ports in the Mediterranean and the Black Sea provided safe havens, and its trade colonies in Egypt, Constantinople and the Holy Land allowed control of resources. Venice had access to the resources of the Adriatic, eastern Mediterranean, Egypt and Black Sea ports. Its markets encompassed the Mediterranean, Europe and England.

The Mongol Empire was the largest contiguous empire in human history from Korea in the east to the shores of the Mediterranean in the west, from Russia in the north to the Chinese island of Hainan in the south. The Mongols did not directly exploit the resources of these territories but obtained annual tribute from the governments of their vassals. The exception was the rule of Kublai Khan which gradually developed Chinese style government of the Yuan Empire.

The empires of China became prosperous once they had control of the fertile regions and the economy was driven by agriculture. The State combined with large landowners to receive the benefits from cultivation by peasant farm laborers. The Chinese Sung Empire stretched initially from the northern Great Wall as far south as the island Hainan. After the invasion of the Jin, the Southern Sung had to recognise that the northern border was the Huang River. The Southern Sung economy expanded internationally. There is no doubt that Chinese culture under the Sung was dominant in China, Korea and Japan. It also influenced countries in South-east Asia. At this period of history there was little flow of Chinese culture to Christian Europe.

For the ancient/medieval period I have identified a pattern of colonial expansion by dominant cultures from areas of limited resources to access, through commercial or military dominance, to the unlimited wealth of a wide geographic region.

The Paradigm of Political Control

The ancient kings of Phoenician city/states were guided by priests and citizen councils who appear during times of peace to have had control of, what we now call "the economy". At times of war, the kings assumed more direct control of the decision making process. There is little, if any, evidence remaining to show that Phoenician society was administered by any bureaucracy, but the pattern of commerce and the use of non-hieroglyphic writing suggest that it would be natural to assume that a form of bureaucracy existed.

The Achaemenid kings of a Persian military society were undoubtedly the leaders of their culture, but their lasting strength was the administration of their widespread realm by the bureaucracy overseen by *satraps*. Fast communication by pony express over the king's roads enabled the monitoring of the administration. Military and civil powers were kept separate to lessen the chances of revolt. This policy was successful until Xerxes returned to Persopolis after defeat in Greece. The later kings isolated themselves in the royal city out of touch with their governors, so that the *satrapies* became more independent and subject to outside interference. The later Persians, Parthians and Sassanids, used some aspects of the Achaemenid government.

The Macedonian Ptolemy I found in Egypt, a priestly bureaucracy which for millennia had been directed by pharaohs, to which he could add a military administration. Although the docility of the Egyptian people themselves was a factor in the colonisation of Egypt by a relatively small military force, it was the administration which enabled the Ptolemies to extract the agricultural wealth of the country. The monetisation of Egyptian commerce through a royal central bank was only made possible by an efficient bureaucracy. The later Ptolemies, who tended to pursue a hedonistic lifestyle in Alexandria, apparently lost control of their administration both in rural regions and in Hellenistic cities.

The Romans developed a cultural hatred of kings so that the Republic advanced under military leaders, who theoretically ruled for short periods of time, but were never called "kings". The guidance of leaders by the Senate, comprised of ex-leaders and patricians, and the establishment of a secondary leadership structure (*praetors, aediles*) provided a stable administration within a military society. The democratic nature of the society caused fractures of the administration when *tribunes* from the popular Assembly disagreed with the oligarchs of the Senate.

Strong men take charge of any fractured administration, so it was natural that Rome returned to a military structure when their civilian leadership was found wanting. It was only the cultural fear of the word "*king*" that stopped the initial leaders of Empire from adopting the title, but the first Emperors were "*kings*" in fact, who ruled through their personal influence over their armies. A stronger bureaucratic administration was built which was then only responsible to the Emperor.

India had a long history of cultural dominance by a defined ruling class which appeared to lead to popular acceptance of strong ruling emperors. Royalty imposed a bureaucracy on empire which was beneficial in golden periods. Religion played a large part in golden periods, although the expansion of Buddhism by

Asoka might have lead to imperial decline. The Cholas continued the rule of a hereditary monarchy with an organised administrative structure.

China experienced waves of invasion by northern barbarian tribes some of whom were gradually absorbed by Chinese culture. It was only when fighting emperors accepted Confucianist bureaucracy that peaceful expansion was enabled. Under the Han, prominence of bureaucrats & palace eunuchs came to the fore, which was to prove characteristic for most of Chinese history. Under Emperor Wu-ti, the traffic on the Silk Road began to flourish as never before. In the period under review, decline mainly occurred through dissention in the ruling class and the large landholders which included many bureaucrats.

The Byzantines maintained the imperial government of the Romans, and their periods of dominance were due to competent emperors such as Justinian I and Heraclius. The imperial government was aided by the Church, and the decline of Byzantium was hastened by the break of the Greek-speaking Orthodox Church from the Roman Catholic Church in 653, at the time of the explosive rise of Islam.

As Islam spread, the Muslim caliphs and *amirs* founded a bureaucratic administration, initially in Greek and Pahlavi languages, but then in Arabic. The Arab Muslim *amirs* initially ruled from armed camps outside existing cities. The previous fervent Arab tribesmen were replaced by a multi-cultural standing army paid by taxes under nearly independent *amirs*. The Abbasid caliphs became more distant from empire and reliant on Turkic-speaking armed forces and then Turkic slaves (*mamluks*). Turkic *amirs* then took over government.

The Catholic Franks ruled as kings with the approval of the Roman Church. The warrior king/emperor could rule with the support of his farmer war bands because of the Germanic tradition binding the men to their leader. Central government was made possible by the administration of the territory by counts (*comes*) who, as vassals, were personally responsible to the king. Central control was made possible by government inspectors (*missi dominici*) solely responsible to the king. The inspectors ensured that the nobles performed their duties to the king's approval. The close association with a pliable Roman Church enhanced the emperor's control. The vassal relationship was personal so that nobles and their vassals obeyed a sole leader. *Charlemagne*, in particular, was a strong Emperor over a united territory administered by his nobles. When the territory became divided, nobles were able to divide loyalty and gradually divorced from the vacillating royalty.

The Holy Roman Emperors had limited control over empire because the German nobles in fact decided whether raise armies to support the Emperor. There was apparently no permanent imperial administration.

By the thirteenth century the kings of Francia had started to regain regal dignity and standing. Louis VII and Philippe *Auguste* in particular gained authority over counts and great lords, with the possible exception of the dukes of Normandy. The king's officials had gained considerable power in their own right. This led to the evolution of a government structure outside the nobility that was dependent on the king.

China endured invasion by northern Toba tribes which were gradually absorbed by Chinese culture. Buddhism was favoured by the Sui emperors to unite China under officials from the landed class. The T'ang Emperors reintroduced Confucian educated bureaucrats who, however, still favoured the landed gentry. The Sung dynasty ruled with Confucian bureaucrats but maintained the peace to the north by expensive tribute to the Khitan Liao. Landowner opposition arose in the twelfth century which in turn led to peasant revolutions. The Emperor became influenced by eunuchs and the army could not repel the *Chin/Jin*. The new Southern Sung dynasty introduced various measures of economic rehabilitation and fiscal reform.

The Norman culture accepted the more civilised influences of the cultures that they conquered, but maintained their warrior control through nobles who evolved into barons. The royal control faded when warrior control lapsed, often because of new cultural influences.

Venice was ruled by an oligarchy of wealthy families led by a Doge (duke) and governed by various councils. State capitalism governed the mercantile trade with financial stabilisation through bonds often covered through forced loans from the wealthy.

Ghengis Khan commenced an administration and law which would allow the governing of the territories conquered by the Mongol armies. He introduced discipline and military units to his growing army. Although Genghis' sons and grandsons followed Ghengis' practice of control to some degree, internecine warfare interfered with sound management of territory. On the death of a *khagan* a successor needed to be elected by the Mongol council (*kuriltai*) from the leading family members.

Ancient and medieval leaders were very diverse in their actions and cultures, but I have identified a common strength in the establishment of able bureaucracies which allowed the relatively just administration of their societies. Peaceful administration in turn provided the basis for prosperity. Each culture went into decline when the leaders no longer could control their bureaucracies. The decline of the cultures tended to stem mainly from internal pressure, which sometimes allowed the fatal fall from external intrusion.

Cohesive Religion

The Phoenicians were thought to have been initially monotheistic, or at least worshipping a small pagan pantheon in a religion which strengthened their society. At times priests actually rose to positions of power, as high as priest/king. The tolerance of the Phoenicians towards religions of peoples with whom they traded, allowed expansion of their own pantheon of gods. El, the great god, lost power in favour of Baal, the son, who then became multi-faceted. The consort, Astarte the fertility goddess, came to possess many aspects of the Babylonian goddess, Ishtar, and the Egyptian Isis.

The early Achaemenid Persians were evidently ambivalent about religion, and Cyrus must have grasped the notion that political power over diverse peoples was made easier if their religions were respected. Cyrus worshipped the Aryan god Ahura Mazda to maintain his Median and Persian base, but accepted other gods when in distant realms. One can assume that Cyrus' embrace of the Babylonian god, Marduk, acceptance of the Jewish god, Yahweh, and Cambyses acceptance of the title "Son of Ra", had political motives. Darius was apparently more devoted to Ahura Mazda than his predecessors, but followed the example of tolerance towards the local gods of the *satrapies*. Xerxes was the first Persian king who failed to respect the local gods of his Empire, and from his time the Persian pantheon expanded. Artaxerxes II is reported to have worshipped Anahita and Mithra, as well as Ahura Mazda.

Ptolemy I had been able to personally observe the respect accorded to Alexander *the Great* when he adopted the persona of the son of Ammon-Zeus, and no doubt was a party to Alexander's use of the powerful organisation of priests whose authority under the pharaohs had been built over millennia. Ptolemy introduced a new god, Serapis, apparently to unite Egyptians and Greeks, but as Akhenaten earlier, and many leaders in the future, were to find, religion could not be imposed. The rural Egyptians and the Greek/Macedonian soldier/settlers preferred their old gods. It was really in the Ptolemies' royal satellite city of Alexandria that Serapis was accepted, and then only as an addition to the pantheon of the old gods. For the majority of the time, pagan Alexandria, the centre of Egyptian commerce and learning, was tolerant about the Jewish religion of the large Hebrew population. The toleration of exotic religions led to ready acceptance of the Greek mystery religions, which coincidentally marked the decline of the Ptolemaic Empire.

Mars, the god of war, was the main Roman god prior to colonisation of the Italian peninsula. The earliest additions to the Roman pantheon were Etruscan and Greek gods from cultures fought and admired by the Romans. The public worship of Juppiter, Juno and Minerva was a political necessity for leaders of the Roman Republic. The chief priest, *pontifex maximus*, had both a religious and secular role. The expansion of the Roman realm to include Greece and Asia Minor caused soldiers and merchants to come into contact with gods of conquered peoples. The introduction to Rome of Cybele, Bacchus and Aphrodite, expanded the Roman pantheon. The Greek mystery religions further splintered Roman religious cohesion, which was put in terminal decline when emperors declared their predecessors as gods.

The first two Mauryan emperors, Chandragupta and Bindusara were reputedly even-handed between Jain and Buddha, although Hindu Jain tradition claims that in the last days of his life Chandragupta was converted to Jainism. Ashoka was converted to Buddhism but respected all the religious sects and encouraged his people to be even-handed. Under the Guptas, Hinduism benefited from royal support and subsidies, and it regained the supremacy that it had lost to Buddhism. Buddhist and Jaina literature which was produced earlier in Prakrit languages began to appear in Sanskrit. The Indian emperors appear to have practiced religious tolerance.

Ancestor worship has been a central point in Chinese religion from the beginnings of civilisation. The Chinese emperors had not only to worship ancestors by costly burials but also to be reverent to natural phenomena like Heaven and Earth, the Great Unity and several deities and spirits according to the seasons. The Emperor was the only one worthy enough to approach the gods. Under the Han, Confucianism became the established philosophy-*cum*-religion of the people. Buddhism entered China during the middle Han period and, after the Han dynasty fell, spread with a missionary zeal to the point where the majority of the population of northern China was Buddhist. Thousands of Buddhist temples were built, with Buddhism becoming the predominant landowner -- analogous to the landholdings of the medieval Catholic Church in Europe. Rising to the challenge, a Taoist Church was established (having little relation to original Taoism). Taoist temples were built which cultivated alchemy, mainly seeking an elixir of immortality, but also contributed to the development of porcelain, medicine and other technologies. The court of Wu-ti not only worshipped the Buddha, but the Emperor protected monasteries and sponsored them.

After a break from the Roman Church, the Byzantines became united by what was becoming Greek Orthodox Christianity. Intolerance of other religions occurred during decline.

Mohammed used force to impose his religion on his countrymen and was supported by a willing army. Islam was the ostensible reason for the Arab conquests. Islam was tolerant of Christian and Jewish religions.

Emperor Wen-ti favoured both Buddhism and Taoism, but later turned to Buddhism which was used to unify the Sui Empire. Li Yuan claimed descent from Laozi but as the first T'ang Emperor Kao-Tsu evenly supported both Taoism and Buddhism. After the T'ang Empress favoured her Buddhist sponsors, Emperor Hsuan-tsung (712-762) showed slight favouritism to Taoism. Emperor Wu-tsung (841-846) was a fervent Taoist. Under him the previous T'ang tolerance of religion was changed to persecution of Manichaeans, Buddhists, Zoroastrians and Nestorians. As least part of this persecution was economically based, particularly against the Buddhists whose land and metals were confiscated for the state. During the Sung dynasty, Neo-Confucianism incorporated some Buddhist and Taoist ideas into Confucian ideology. Many historians believe that the rigid Confucian orthodoxy of government after 1200, fossilised Chinese culture up to the twentieth century.

Under Pippin *the Short*, the Carolingian Catholic Church was organised and united under the direction of the king. *Charlemagne* insisted on organisation of parish and diocese supervised by the bishop. The bishops, under the authority of the archbishops, were still nominated by the Emperor, generally from the nobility. Before Louis *the Pious*, Frank leaders had justified the Church as a corporate and juristic body which used religious faith to unify a diversified collection of families, tribes, and conquered peoples under canon law applied by a just king. Under Louis, the bishops developed political and theological theory - political Augustinianism - that the bishops were superior to kings who were simply responsible for the protection of the Church and State. The Frank Church then suffered from lack of royal protection which meant the powerful barons came to appoint ecclesiastical officers as a feudal right. Monasteries had become secular communities which had lost much of their spiritual life.

The Cholas promoted the Hindu religion and the era saw religious revival in both Saiva and Vaishnava traditions. Due to the caste system, Hinduism appealed more to upper echelons than the common people. Late in empire, Islam became a force which threatened Hinduism.

The Holy Roman Empire commenced as a partnership between the Pope and the Emperor. A number of Popes chafed as inferior members of the partnership until Gregory VII exercised strong papal authority. When the Pope intervened in investitures by kings, Germany accelerated its lapse into separate principalities.

Suger, abbot of St. Denis, was an important official in King Louis VI's French administration which became closer to the Roman Catholic Church. A number of Popes were able to claim refuge in France, and even towns and churches outside the royal demesne appealed for Louis' protection.

The Normans accepted Roman Catholicism from their European conquests and supported their religion particularly against Islam. Russia accepted Greek Orthodox religion from Byzantium. Like other royalty of the age, Norman English kings had problems with popes over lay investiture of bishops within their realm.

The Venetians were basically as Catholic as the rest of Europe, but the religion was more relaxed in the commercial empire without apparent dominance from the Church of Rome.

The Mongols followed animistic religions under a shaman. The first *khagans* were tolerant of the religions of their realm but when others converted to Islam there were internecine problems. Kubilai converted to Buddhism but was tolerant of other religions.

The names of gods, and methods of worship suggest a wide diversity of ancient religion, however many of the gods of different cultures had common attributes. If one takes a broad view of the religious pattern without examining the religions themselves, one can see the political importance of religious cohesion to the culture of a society which is rising to prominence. Medieval religion was not as diverse as those of the ancient pagans but a battle for religious dominance had commenced.

A dominant society necessarily comes into contact with other cultures, and as a mature civilisation tends to become tolerant of the religions of those cultures. Coincident with decline as a dominant culture, the old religion was diluted with the embrace of new gods. It is as if the acceptance of new religious ideas accompanied the questioning of the old political regime.

Innovation and Advances in Technology

The expansion of the Phoenician maritime trading empire was made possible by the introduction of a commercial vessel capable of relatively deep sea voyages. It is a moot point whether the original design was adapted and improved from the more ancient Sea Peoples. The production of purple dye was an idea possibly stolen from another culture, but it was the Phoenicians who improved the process to the point where it was the basis of a major textile industry. Opaque glass manufacture had been carried out by the Babylonians and Egyptians, but it was the commercial foresight of the Phoenicians which stimulated the development of clear glass. It is likely that the need for commercial records was the motive for improvement of the Aramaean alphabet into running writing that was then taught by the Phoenicians to their widespread trading empire, including Greece.

It is my contention that the Achaemenid Persian domination was made possible because of a fine civil/military administration through *satraps*. The initial military conquests were apparently made possible through efficient organisation of soldiers rather than by the introduction of new weapons, although weapon technology was improved when the Persians enveloped the decaying Assyrian empire. The origin of governors to run provinces might well have been Assyrian, but the *satrap* administration was refined by Cyrus and expanded by Darius with communication by pony express. Without an efficient bureaucracy, the logistics of the huge army that Xerxes raised to invade Europe, would not have been possible. Money was not invented by the Persians, but its use to bribe and foment unrest within enemy societies, appears to have been a Persian innovation, later followed by the Greeks.

Ptolemy I *Soter* recognised the worth of technology by importing superior Greek agricultural practices and drainage techniques to improve Egyptian agricultural output as the basis for royal wealth. *Soter* created the Great Library and Museum, possibly to attract the great thinkers of the age from the known world. Under Ptolemy II *Philadelphus*, new Hellenistic philosophies and technology were produced which provided the foundations for future European societies.

Rome's farmers/soldiers adapted the Etruscan/Greek military techniques to suit their colonial expansion of the Italian peninsula. They learned from any battle losses, by adapting their military technology to ensure that similar losses did not re-occur. International conflict with large bodied Celts, and Pyrrhic elephants, caused major formation and weapon reorganisation. The greatest advance was to build a navy in response to the threat from maritime Carthage, by using Punic vessels as a model, and training crews on land. The technological advance of the "raven" which gave the Romans the edge on shore-close naval conflict was an adaptation of an earlier Greek weapon. As the Romans expanded throughout the Mediterranean, their military commanders utilised any foreign technology which could assist their command. The later famous Roman thrusting broad-sword was developed in Spain, and missile throwing weapons came from Asia.

Sculptural finds from the Indian Mauryan period indicate that sculptors of that time had achieved a high degree of proficiency in working with stone. They had tools and implements that enabled them to create smoothly modelled and highly polished representations of human and animal figures. The Mauryans had good military technology and minted coins. The Gupta period is accepted as the birth-time of several mathematical concepts, including zero, the decimal system, algorithm, square root and cube root. Gupta astronomers also made advances in astronomy by using their mathematical breakthroughs. The bow was the dominant weapon of the Gupta army. The Hindu version of the longbow was composed of metal, or more typically bamboo, and fired a long bamboo cane arrow with a metal head. Due to its high tensility, the steel bow was capable of long range and penetration of exceptionally thick armor.

The Chinese Han state guided production of salt and iron, coin casting (in Han China, coins were caste, not minted), the production of iron tools and of standard weights and measures. The compass, and the seismograph were invented in the Han period, and the wheelbarrow was a mundane technological innovation. Taoist alchemists used saltpetre mixed with sulphur as incendiaries. The earliest forms of paper were made from bamboo fibre and used as clothing in the early years of the Han, but by the late Han period true paper was being used for writing. Fine porcelain dates from Han times. The government controlled water-ways and water supply for agriculture.

The Byzantines were under continual pressure from invaders so that little new technology appeared in the early medieval period.

The Muslim warriors adapted the technology of the cultures that they conquered, and quickly developed naval skills. Paper was introduced from China which led to translation of knowledge from ancient Greek, Egyptian and Indian books into Arabic paper books. By 825 the Indians' advanced decimal calculating techniques using nine characters and zero were in Arab use. Alchemy, the forerunner to modern chemistry, was refined from practices in ancient Egypt by Muslim scientists. Following the Greek scientific approach in the eighth century, Jabir ibn Hayyan introduced a methodical and experimental approach to alchemy. One of the Greek inventions that Islam elaborated and spread was the astrolabe which could determine latitude, sunrise and sunset, and which allowed expansion of maritime trade. The Umayyad dynasty did much to improve the cultural knowledge of Spain and Europe from the Muslim translation of many ancient Greek and Indian books. Some of this knowledge passed to northern Europe. There does not appear to be any Islamic native evolution of technology, but there was fine implementation of past ideas.

The Catholic Franks also adopted technology from other cultures rather than invent their own. The stirrup which came from the Far East was adapted to allow an improved cavalry of Frank nobles. The German heavy plough was introduced to replace the lighter Romano-Celt plough.

The innovation of the medieval Holy Roman Empire was the change to vassalage by Conrad II which allowed a number of nobles the inheritance rights to land in Italy and Germany.

To the earlier Chinese inventions of the mariner's compass, sternpost rudder, and printing press, the Sung period added man-powered paddle-wheelers, water-powered textile machinery and the use of firearms in warfare (c1200). The Sung dynasty was the first in the world to issue paper printed money as banknotes, although this proved to be a mixed blessing. Coal was introduced as a fuel for smelter blast furnaces which could produce 100,000 tonnes of iron product per year. Most iron was for military use but expansion of the canal system expanded the use of iron products throughout China.

The Normans were enamoured of castles which they improved in France and introduced to England. English technological innovations of the twelfth century included nailed horseshoes, horse collars, and tandem harnesses, which improved agriculture. Watermills and windmills powered machine based processing. It is reasonable to assume that wheeled iron ploughs drawn by oxen teams were introduced to England from France by some Norman landowners.

Venice was quick to use any innovation from other cultures. The standout technological advantage came from the state-controlled Arsenal which repaired and built ships to order from the State and merchants. A number of financial innovations assisted the mercantile trade.

The Mongol warriors adopted any new weapons to assist their conquests, including siege machines and fire rockets. The Mongols did not invent paper money but issued it, with the normal consequences of excessive printing. They conducted a census of their realm to allow taxation.

In my opinion, the advance of "golden cultures" was not due to the invention of new technology, but often the innovative adaptation of earlier, or foreign technology. In many respects this would be natural because the advance of these societies was due to organised pursuit of their aims, which might not have encouraged the individualism that is, more often than not, responsible for technological breakthroughs. The improvement of technology through the ages has often taken place within an organisational framework. The common pattern in the cultures under review is the enthusiastic embrace of technology which could be adapted to suit the leaders' vision of progress. Decline often was accompanied by lack of will or wealth to pursue further technological innovation.

The Rule of Law

Although I am not aware of evidence that the Phoenician culture enjoyed the rule of law, it is unlikely that an organised commercial culture could be sustained for centuries without some form of legal structure. The export of the Phoenician alphabet throughout the Mediterranean, as well as contact with Babylon and Egypt, suggests to me that codified laws might have existed in a physical form that did not endure the millennia before archaeological efforts.

The Achaemenid Persian governors implemented local laws in the outreaches of Empire, as long as those laws did not countermand royal Persian law. It was up to the *satrap* to enforce both the king's, and local regulations, through local magistrates where necessary. The king was the ultimate magistrate and his word was law. The early Achaemenid kings were sufficiently politically astute to ensure that their word did not deviate too far from accepted cultural practice.

Ptolemy I *Soter* came to control an Egyptian society regulated by priests and magistrates that had enforced the pharaohs' will. The bureaucratic administration then codified the Macedonian and Greek regulations into law that co-existed with, but commended, Egyptian regulation/laws. The later Ptolemies were unable to enforce their regulation/law in rebellious rural areas and fractious Alexandria.

The Romans were obsessed with laws on the basis that democratic law would ensure that kings could not rule their society by the law of decree. In theory a republic can only exist when the people who elect the governing officials, can be confident that those officials will follow the rule of law, known and accepted by the majority of the people. In fact, the laws produced by the Roman Senate could be as confusing and contradictory as any decrees produced by ancient kings, and not until late in the Republic was codified law produced.

A further protection against tyranny was the Roman jury system which allowed trial by the people, of those who broke the laws of the people. *Praetors* acted as magistrates to enforce most laws, and their decisions were not subject to appeal. Political influence meant that juries were initially controlled by Senators and then *equites*, until the people's representative tribunes forced wider representation. When the law was abused by the ruling class, strong individuals arose to introduce their own interpretation of the law with military backing to introduce the imperial culture.

The Indian Mauryan Empire was divided into four provinces, with the imperial capital at Pataliputra. The head of the provincial administration was the *kumara* (royal prince), who governed the provinces as king's representative. The *kumara* was assisted by *mahamatyas* and council of ministers. This organisational structure was reflected at the imperial level with the Emperor and his *Mantriparishad* (Council of Ministers). The law applied was on the basis of ancient religious texts, and was administered by the emperors under advice of ministers and learned Brahmins. The emperor also appointed judges to administer the law. Law at the village level was administered by a village or caste *panchayat* consisting of 5 or more members. State law then appears to have been on Hindu religious precedent under royal or administration edict, as was common in a military society. In the Gupta period, the governors of the provinces were more independent as compared to the Mauryans but administration of the law appears the same.

The Chinese Emperor was traditionally bound to obedience of natural law and had the duty as "Son of Heaven" to define manifest law and when it was broken. The Emperor's court would punish the breach. The Han Confucionists recognised that the emperor had paramount power over all facets of life, including law. The Han dynasty formally recognised four sources of law: *lü* ("codified laws"), *ling* ("the emperor's order"), *ke* ("statutes inherited from previous dynasties") and *bi* ("precedents"), among which *ling* has the highest binding power over the other three. Most legal professionals were not lawyers but generalists trained in philosophy and literature. The local, classically trained, Confucian gentry played a crucial role as arbiters and handled all but the most serious local disputes.

Sharia law was introduced by the Muslim culture which overrode the ancient laws of the conquered territory. The new laws, linked to religion, were treated seriously. Trial by jury was possible and the Islamic jury, called *Lafif*, consisted of twelve members from the district who were bound to give a unanimous verdict. Some say that the *Latif* might have been introduced to England by the Crusaders so that it might have influenced English law.

Charlemagne was advised by experts in the groups of laws effective throughout empire, as well as Roman and Byzantine law. A council took place in which the king participated. After agreement, the law was drafted as a royal decree. Royal commands, called capitularies, were issued listing *Charlemagne's* decrees point by point. There were two tribunals - the king's tribunal and the count's tribunal, initially obligatory to be attended by all freemen. The count's tribunal under Charlemagne had a prosecuting count as sole judge. When there was a suit involving a number of claimants the counts had advisors of important citizens which later involved into seven professional judges trained in law.

Chola justice was administered by regularly constituted royal courts in addition to village courts. Crimes of the state, such as treason, were dealt with the king himself. The most striking feature of the Chola period was the unusual vigour and efficiency of the autonomous rural institutions.

The kings of France were able to extend their authority because professional government and law had been introduced. The use of the words "*fief*" and "*homage*" to indicate political subjection appears to have developed in France in the same time frame as the subjection appears in Lombardy, as a result of the law schools in Montpellier and Bologna.

The use of a Confucian bureaucracy meant that the legal code under the Sung was based on that of the earlier T'ang dynasty. Official magistrates were expected to be well versed in written law, but there was also the expectation that they ensure a moral society.

The Norman kings of England professed to rule by the Anglo-Saxon customary laws of Edward *the Confessor* with some additions of their own. The innovation added to criminal law was the murder fine (*murdrum*) which made the fine for murder payable by the community if the murderer could not be produced. Another Norman introduction to England was the "appeal" whereby the injured party or his near relation could prove the charge of felony by battle. By 1166, a precursor to trial by jury became the standard. However, this group of "twelve lawful men," provided a service more similar to a modern American grand jury, alerting court officials to matters suitable for prosecution. The famous Magna Carta was not really a document about rights; it was a document about limiting the power of the king.

The role in Venetian law by the Doge and his councils was strong but relatively tolerant.

Genghis Khan created a code of laws (*yasak*) which were relatively simple but provided an orderly society. The penalty for breaking the law was often death.

The common thread linking "golden cultures" was a respect by the cultures' leaders for the rule of regulation or law that was culturally known, if not necessarily approved, by the people. The laws, and their enforcement, were not always fair and just, because, as in modern civilisation, leaders tended to interpret laws to favour political will. On balance however, the leaders' desire for a well regulated society meant that laws were made with an eye to acceptable precedent and enforced to produce an orderly society.

Government Risk Management - Advance or Decline

One cannot properly assess the risk management of an ancient society as Phoenicia with so much history unknown, but my theory would be that a non-military trading culture would always be vulnerable to a culture dominated by thirst for conquest. It appears that the Assyrians were the first to pollute the Phoenician culture through military domination. The first Assyrian kings were relatively benign to the Phoenician confederation, but they did demand tributes, so that independence of the city/states was lost. Maybe the Phoenicians did recognise that their culture needed to be preserved in the colonies. Apparently Carthage grew in stature at the same time as the Phoenician maritime empire declined, so that a number of previously Phoenician colonies became Carthaginian. Carthage became the major power in the western Mediterranean until conflict with the Romans.

The rise of the Persian Empire was based on the acquisition and improvement of territory and ideas from other cultures. The early *Achaemenid* monarchs were conscious of the risks of opposition to their rule, but had access to huge resources from their military empire to be comfortable in managing any risk. After Xerxes, his successors recognised the risk posed by the Greeks and developed a new way to use their resources to provide risk management. For possibly the first time in the world, one government tried to assert international influence on other national governments through money. Gold and money was used to bribe and intrigue infighting between the Greek city/states so that a unified force could not be raised against Persia. The success of this policy was seen in the Peloponnesian Wars 431-404BC, when Persian finance assisted Sparta against Athens.

The later *Achaemenid* rulers were too pre-occupied with the royal lifestyle to be able to deal adequately with internal division, let alone decide on defensive fortifications against an invasion from Europe. In many respects, the later failure of Persian risk management was a result of natural dynastic decline.

Without the victories from aggressive expansion, the large Ptolemaic navy was no doubt expensive, and it was allowed to decline under Ptolemy *Philopator*. Unfortunately this allowed others to weaken Egypt's outlying influence, so that there were few buffers against aggression by the time Roman naval power became dominant. The later Ptolemies lost their independence before they lost Egypt because internal dissent had taken away their power. The later Ptolemaic generations either failed through lack of military intelligence to see, or lacked the ability to counter, outside threats to Egyptian independence. At the end, Cleopatra's forces, as Antony's allies, showed that the Egyptian military (with mercenaries) could be a force to be reckoned with, but her predecessors had lacked the will.

Republican Rome's great early strength was its military society in which the army of soldier settlers provided not only the expansion and defence of the borders, but the backbone which unified the classes with purpose. Each class was militarily oriented to willingly perform their duties to other classes. The rank and file were farmers who fought with commendable zeal and returned to their small holdings to till the soil after military engagements. Risk from outside the Roman Republic was well recognised, and the military society generally coped well early when the wars were on Italian soil. It was the need to send armies overseas, the establishment of a competent navy, and the continuous wars that expanded Roman realms, but weakened the domestic cohesion of the military society.

The success of external risk management over foreign cultures caused of the erosion of the cohesive domestic culture of Roman honour. The risk to the Roman Republic was within, and went unrecognised until the leading generals had already commenced their civil wars. The leaders of the Senate and the Assembly were too concerned with their private welfare to recognise the risk that their own lack of honour would inspire similar selfishness among the urban mob. In such a situation it was only natural that a strong general would seek to impose his own version of discipline on a disturbed society. It was also only natural that other ambitious generals would oppose the imposed leadership of their colleagues. Peace returned only when Octavian Augustus introduced Empire, as a class dominated society in which fortunes were acquired by the privileged few from militarily imposed regulation of the oppressed many.

The Roman army was needed in Empire, not only to defend the borders but to ensure an orderly provincial society that paid its share of the growing burden of imperial taxes. An increasing level of taxes was needed to finance the huge military budget and to a lesser extent, to pay for imported grain to feed Rome and Italy. The growing civil service, necessary to collect taxes, itself became a large expense to Empire. The knightly class, who had been the *publicanii* (tax-farmers), came to dominate the Ministry of Finance, and the civil service. The specialised civil servant tended not to have had military service, and, when the separation of military and civil careers was complete under Hadrian, the civil service was able to be dominated by the army. Individuals and states throughout Empire were forced into debt to pay taxes - *debt before dishonour.*

By the early medieval period the Byzantine Empire was an empire in name only surrounded by hostile forces that it could not control. Decline that had started in past ages could not be reversed.

The Chinese Sui dynasty was brought to its economic knees by the Emperor Yang-ti (581-618) who was obsessed with the domination of Korea. The arrogance of the emperor was again rewarded with a peasant uprising from which the T'ang dynasty arose. The T'ang continued relatively good governance until China's first empress usurped the throne. Empress Wu Zhao was able to rise from concubine due to weakness of the court, with support from Buddhist clergy. She ruled only for 15 years but she weakened the power of the north-west aristocracy which allowed later rebellions and invasions.

The failure of Sung imperial forces to recover Beijing from the invading *Chin/Jin*, together with the economy, apparently turned the Sung Dynasty away from warlike policies. The settlement of tributes on the Chin to stop any invasion further south, allowed the emperors to neglect the military in favour of literature and art. The final Southern Sung ruler was another cultured emperor who had placed his faith in politicians rather than his generals so was unprepared when the Mongols resumed their attack upon southern China. Kublai Khan was eventually successful in completely crushing the Sung by 1279.

The Muslim Caliphates laid the seed for their own destruction because the Arab armies, on which their success depended, could not be sustained when there were no new territories available to conquer. By the early ninth century the Muslim army was dependent on slaves (*mamluks*), Turkish mercenaries, Slavs and Berbers. The Turks gradually established political control and were able to influence the establishment of provincial governors who assumed caliphate power in their regions. By the 870s the Abbasid caliphs were in thrall to the Turkish party and reigned in name only. The Muslim leaders had failed to maintain cultural integrity.

Royal patrimony was apparently the root cause of weakness to the Frank kingdom. The early Carolingians were lucky in many respects that premature deaths did not cause division of their territory more than the Merovingian divide of Neustria (approximately modern France) and Austrasia (approximately modern Germany). *Charlemagne* reunited the territory as empire but his surviving son Louis *the Pious* caused division between his sons and nobles. The empire had basically collapsed due to dynastic infighting before Louis *the Pious* died in 840.

The Chola Empire at its peak was subjected to wars with the Chalukyas who had previously controlled central India and the Pandyas who had fled to Sri Lanka. Finally, some enemies used Muslim administrators and mercenaries to have more success. The later Chola emperors lacked the vigour to attack their enemies to force capitulation, and gradually the continued defence wore away Chola control. The Cholas appear to be the only culture indentified as falling due to outside influence, but not enough is known of possible royal weakness within.

The Holy Roman Empire was always in danger of collapse because there was no central government. The Emperor had to encourage princes and nobles through words or bribery to support his measures to endeavour to control empire.

Norman rule was weakened by patrimony because of the plans by Henry II to divide his kingdom. The battles between Henry's sons before the king died, allowed interference by Philippe II of France which continued even after Richard was crowned King of England. John Lackland lost territory to France which was not able to be retrieved by future English kings. Succession problems were also at the heart of decline in Sicily and Russia. The kingdom of France was on the rise after Philippe II *Auguste* but was in danger from the English Normans. The decline of Norman Empire allowed the rise of France.

The closely packed city of Venice was devastated by plague which caused a great loss of native seamen. The main cause of the Venetian decline appears to be the failure of the mercantile fleet to maintain its dominance because imported crews lacked the skills of their predecessors. This weakness occurred at the same time that the Ottomans gained maritime skills.

The dominant cultures under review appear to have had such diverse societies that it is difficult to summarise their methods of management to avoid the risk of disintegration or defeat. At first glance the diversity would appear to suggest that there was no commonality between the various cultures' failure to identify risk and thus failure to manage risk. However if one takes the broad view, it is possible to say that a common feature of mature "golden cultures" was an arrogance of leadership which did not allow for the thought of defeat of empire.

Secondly, the arrogance was to a degree justified because the decline which ended each culture's dominance of its age, did not come directly from outside its society. The introduction of ideas from other cultures, acceptable because of the mature enlightened tolerance of secure leaders, caused an insidious dilution of cultural identity. Each "golden culture" was not conquered by another dominant culture until it was already weakened by the decay caused by internal erosion of heritage cultural values.

In all the aforementioned societies, the initial leaders had the exuberance to forge their people into a proud regulated confederation that could dominate other cultures. When each generation of rulers became incrementally less imbued with the old values, the driving factor came to be the retention/improvement of the wealth/power of the ruling class, rather than the advancement of the society as a whole.

The accent of later leaders towards hedonism, coincident with the absorption of outside influences by the general population, provided the fertile ground for the disintegration of each society. I suspect that an exponential increase in leadership debt accompanied the rise in hedonism, but this cannot be proven in the early cultures.

Conclusion - There is a Cyclical Pattern

In Chapter 1, I explained the cyclical concept, and in particular the long term climatic cycle as hypothesised by Dr. Raymond Wheeler and others. I have sought to demonstrate in this chapter that the rhythm of ancient history harmonically produces the "up-and-down" beat in the symphony of civilised progress. To demonstrate that rhythms have occurred throughout millennia, I had to indicate a reasonable commonality in the factors of time, resources, leadership, religion, technology and law.

The pattern of each dominant society shows a rhythm in phase with those of past cultures, but there is no incontrovertible proof that this rhythm exists. I, and many intelligent men, present and past, believe that the rhythm does exist as a cycle of human conduct. I hope that my research has been able to convince the reader that the long term cyclical theory of human progress is credible.

Although proof might not be clearly apparent of ancient cycles, one can still state an assumption that if the rhythm is that of human nature, then it should be still occurring. One method of establishing the credibility of long term cyclical theory is to use the ancient rhythm to suggest the course of present day history, and forecast the possible future of the current dominant society.

In the next chapters I will briefly examine the course of the dominant cultures 1400-2100AD. The dominant culture of the twenty-first century, the republic of the United States of America, has indicated some patterns similar to historical cultures. Those patterns can produce some forecasts for the third millennium AD.

"Plus ça change, plus c'est la même chose."
(The more it changes, the more it remains the same)

French Proverb

CHAPTER 3

The Social Pattern of Non-Democratic Nations in the Early Capitalist Era 1400 -1700AD

Dominant Cultures' Common Features in Modern Times

Following my book "**Life/Death Rhythms of Ancient Empires**", I have continued to seek the existence of just and prosperous societies that endured for longer than the life-span of one or two great rulers. I define such a society as one which utilises the resources of its citizens to produce a comfortable way of life with suitable public infrastructure for the majority, as well as to husband surpluses and safeguard reserves to provide relief in times of change. As in ancient and medieval times, dominant cultures that I have identified did not necessarily provide a comfortable way of life for all of its citizens but by and large the way of life for the majority improved over the life of the regime.

I have continued my formula of six factors mentioned in Chapter 2, which need to be present for my benchmark of dominant cultural success:-

1. Climate and geographic access to sustainable resources.
2. A strong leadership structure with just sharing of society's surplus that encourages involvement in peaceful advances, as well as defence/war.
3. A cohesive religion that is tolerant of secular innovation
4. Use of technology to produce and protect prosperity.
5. Codified broadcast laws, capable of being enforced to ensure order.
6. The ability to safeguard civil and cultural integrity in war and peace.

The best of these cultures have given historians the "golden ages" when civilisation thrived

If Dr. Raymond Wheeler's hypothesis held true that "golden ages" throughout history have occurred within every second 100 year climatic cycle, then a pattern should be able to be identified in the dominant cultures that I outline. Of course, I am aware that patterns, like beauty, are often in the eye of the beholder, rather than being immediately self-evident. I do not expect all academic historians to agree with my opinions, and it will be up to the readers to decide whether the patterns that I identify are similarly perceptible to their eye.

Patterns of Geographic Access to Resources 1400-1900

Moscow (Muscovy) overcame surrounding provinces Suzdal 1441-60; Novgorod (1478); Yaroslavl (1463), Rostov (1474) and Tver (modern Kalinin) in 1485; Chernigov, Starodub, Novgorod-Seversky (1503); Pskov (1510) Smolensk (1512) Volokolamsk (1513) Ryazan (1521) and Novgorod-Seversky (1522). Ivan IV defeated and annexed the Khanate of Kazan on the middle Volga in 1552 and later the Astrakhan Khanate, where the Volga meets the Caspian Sea. These victories transformed Russia into a multi-ethnic state.

The Chinese Ming Emperor Hongwu gradually regained the northern provinces of China from the Mongols and destroyed their ability to make war by 1382. The dynasty then took over the southern territory of China.

The Habsburg family grew to European prominence when Maximilian I became Holy Roman Emperor. The Habsburgs expanded their resources mainly though marriage which led to control of the Holy Roman Empire and Spain. Spain then dominated the New World due to papal bulls of Spanish Pope Alexander VI *Borja* that allowed exploitation of gold and silver. Following the discovery in 1521 by Magellan of the Philippines the archipelago became Spanish. When Felipe II claimed the throne of Portugal the Portuguese Empire became Spanish.

The first Ottoman ruler, Osman I successfully dominated Anatolia except for coastal regions. The son Orhan I expanded north-west so that Byzantium was nearly enclosed. Murad I conquered Adrianople (*Edirne*) and expanded into the Balkans and Serbia nearly to Belgrade. Bayezid I conquered Bulgaria and Northern Greece. The Ottomans annexed Serbia but were turned back from Belgrade in 1440. Mehmed II placed the Balkan Peninsula south of the Danube under his direct rule. Constantinople was captured 1453. The Black Sea and Crimea were brought under Turk control which destroyed the Black Sea colonies of Genoa and the Greeks. By 1501 Bayezid II was in control of the whole Peloponnese. The Ottomans annexed the entire Egyptian sultanate, from Syria and Palestine in Sham, to Hejaz in the Arabian Peninsula, and ultimately Egypt itself. Suleiman *the Lawgiver* conquered Belgrade, capital of Hungary, in August 1521. The island of Rhodes was captured from the *Hospitallers*. Suleiman took Baghdad from the Persians in 1535 which gave him control of Mesopotamia and naval access to the Persian Gulf.

By 1510 Safavid Shah Isma'il subdued the geographical area of Persia and the territories of the old Sassanid Empire (224-651AD), including Mesopotamia with the capital of Baghdad. At its zenith, during the long reign of Shah Abbas I the empire's reach, comprised Iran, Iraq, Armenia, Azerbaijan Georgia, and parts of Turkmenistan, Uzbekistan, Afghanistan, Pakistan, and Turkey.

By 1259 France had gained Normandy, Anjou, Maine, Touraine, and Poitou from England. After 1284 Philippe IV *the Fair* controlled Champagne and Brie. The international Fairs of Champagne provided trade and income for France. In 1453 France regained Aquitaine and Louis XI was able to purchase the counties of Roussillon and Perpignan. Brittany was incorporated in 1532. France was united. France claimed Newfoundland in 1524. Francis I colonised Canada by founding Montreal in 1535 for the Catholic faith. In the Caribbean, Guadeloupe and Martinique were settled by *Compagnie des Îles de l'Amérique* in 1635. St. Lucia 1643, St. Martin 1648, St. Barts 1648, Grenada 1649, and St. Croix 1650 followed.

In 1554/55 the Mughal Humayun reconquered North India from Lahore in the west to Jaunpur in the east. In 1558/64 under Akbar, the Punjab, and kingdoms Gwalior, northern Rajputana, Malwa and Gondwana were annexed. The capital was moved from Delhi to Agra. Over the course of Akbar's conquest of Malwa in 1562, he brought most of present-day Rajasthan, Gujarat and Bengal under his control. In the next decade all of those states were brought under total Mughal control. The 1580s saw Kashmir, Multan and Sind annexed. Bengal then came under Mughal control (1576). Then followed Kashmir (1586), Orissa (1592,) Sindh and Baluchistan (1590-1595). In 1636 the Mughals, under Shah Jahan, signed a treaty with the two major Deccan houses – Adil Shahs of Bijapur and Qitb Shahs of Golconda. Aurangzeb annexed Kuch Bihar in North Bengal and subdued most of Assam. He pushed north-west into the Punjab and also drove south, reasserting authority on two further Muslim kingdoms the Adil Shahis of Bijapur (1686) and Qutb Shahis of Golkonda (1687) — to add to the defeat of the Ahmednagar Sultanate that had been accomplished in 1636 while he had been viceroy of the Deccan.

Japan is different from other dominant cultures in that the areas that the feudal Tokugawa Shogunate dominated were simply the relatively small territory of the islands of Japan. Odo Nobunaga and Toyotomi Hideyoshi defeated the *daimyos* (landholding magnates) to consolidate the provinces of Japan into a national feudal military government. They ushered in over two hundred years of relative peace, much of which was in relative isolation from the rest of the world.

In 1579 the Treaty of Utrecht founded the Republic of the Seven United Provinces which included Holland, Zeeland, Utrecht and Groningen. Guelders, Friesland, Drenth, Brabant, later joined together with individual cities - Ghent, Ypres, Antwerp, Breda and Brussels. The Dutch East India Company (*Vereenigde Oost-Indische Compagnie, VOC)* was formed in 1602 with the ability to declare war. Batavia, Indonesia, was established in 1619. Cape Town was occupied 1621, South Africa, was established in 1652, Colombo, Sri Lanka, captured 1658. VOC trading posts were also established in Persia, Bengal, Malacca, Siam, China, Formosa (now Taiwan), as well as the Malabar and Coromandel coasts in India. New Amsterdam in North America, was founded 1614.

Ducal Prussia passed to the senior Hohenzollern branch, the ruling Margraves of Brandenburg, in 1618, and Polish sovereignty over the duchy ended in 1657. Friedrich I achieved the elevation of the duchy to the Kingdom of Prussia in 1701. The former ducal lands became known as East Prussia. Royal Prussia was annexed from the Polish-Lithuanian Commonwealth by the Kingdom of Prussia in 1722. Prussian gains in the Silesian Wars led to the formation of the Province of Silesia in 1740. The newly annexed Royal Prussia and Warmia became the Province of West Prussia, while the Duchy of Prussia (along with part of Warmia) became the Province of East Prussia. Following the second and third partitions (1793–1795), the new Prussian annexations became the Provinces of New Silesia, South Prussia, and New East Prussia, with the Netze District redivided between West and South Prussia. After Prussia's victory in the 1866 Austro-Prussian War, territories annexed by Prussia were reorganised into three new provinces: Hanover, Hesse-Nassau and Schleswig-Holstein. The German Empire was established from the unification of Germany in 1871.

All cultures examined 1400-1900 had more than sufficient resources and territory to maintain dominance for their period under the sun.

The Paradigm of Political Control of Dominant Cultures 1400-1900

Rurik Dynasty Russia 1398-1598

Ivan Vasiliyevich was co-regent with his father in the 1450s and succeeded him in 1462 as Ivan III, Grand Duke/Prince of Moscow. He led a compact and powerful state which cautiously expanded during his long reign. Ivan III took to the field against Novgorod in 1470 and soundly defeated his opposition. Novgorod was forced to sue for peace and pay war indemnities. After further military action in 1477, Novgorod finally recognised Ivan's direct rule over the city in 1478. Ivan III *the Great's* refusal to share the spoils with his brothers caused a number of civil wars in which Ivan was victorious. Ivan introduced a rule that the domains of all his kinsmen should revert on death to the reigning grand duke. In 1480 Ivan refused to pay the customary annual tribute to Khan Ahmed of the Great Horde. In 1492 the death of Casimir IV of Poland fractured the alliance between Poland and Lithuania. Ivan took advantage of the situation to raid Lithuania then under Casimir's son, Prince Alexander of Lithuania. Alexander had to negotiate a peace which ceded twenty towns to Muscovy. The government of Russia became autocratic when Ivan III no longer consulted his *boyars* (leading aristocracy) on affairs of state.

Gavriil Ivanovich became co-regent with his father in 1502 and succeeded in 1505 as Vasili III. In 1510 the concept of Moscow as the *"Third Rome"* was mentioned by the monk Philotheos of Pskov who suggested to Vasili that two Romes had fallen but the third stood in Moscow. In this way the title of Russian Tsar (*Caesar*) was extended from the claim of Ivan III *the Great* to be Tsar of the Rus'. The Holy Roman Emperor Maximilian offered Vasili the title of king which was refused, and Maximilian rejected the imperial title that Vasili wished to adopt.

Grand Prince Ivan IV of Moscow became the pawn of *boyars* but expressed his independence by arranging the murder of one of his overseers when he was thirteen. He commenced his own rule in 1547 when crowned by the Metropolitan as Tsar of all Russia. The period 1547-1560 was really dominated by the Chosen Council of *boyars*. Service to the state was made compulsory for many landowners, particularly hereditary and vassal. The *sudebnik* (law code) tried to regulate movement of peasants between estates due to a shortage of labour. Coupled with the decline of commerce in rural centres, the restrictions on social mobility and labour meant that Russia moved economically in the opposite direction to Europe. Europe had a growing middle class. Ivan's policy was to have an elite class and the others, with no middle class. Ivan responded to a Hanseatic League boycott of his river port, Narva, by inviting the English Muscovy Company to trade through Arkhangelsk on the White Sea in 1553. Ivan granted the privilege of tax-free trade to the English in his major cities. One moderating influence on Ivan was his wife Anastasia who bore him six children. When she died in 1560 Ivan's behaviour became erratic, and paranoid. The drought/famine of the 1560s at a time of Polish-Lithuanian raids, Tatar invasions and sea blockades by the Swedes and Hanseatic League, devastated Russia. In 1570 the plague killed thousands in Moscow. Ivan's anger at the German barons of Livonia caused him to leave Moscow for Alexandrov. He returned to Moscow only when the boyars agreed to absolute rule. In 1565 he set up a court (*oprichnina*) with special powers for a 6000 strong private army of fanatics (*oprichniki*) to strike down the Tsar's enemies. In 1569-70, Ivan's forces, led by the *oprichniki*, sacked Pskov and Novgorod. Apparently Ivan's paranoia saw threats from the mercantile foreign trade of Novgorod which resulted in the death of thousands through unusually painful methods. Novgorod was never able to recover prosperity after the massacre. It is quite possible that Ivan's mental illness was in full flight at this time. It is the orgy of terror that gained Ivan his nickname "*the Terrible*" from the Russian "*Grozny*" - although this should translate to "*formidable*" or "*fearsome*".

Tsar Ivan IV *Grozny* died, most possibly of poison, and left the ravaged Russia to his possibly retarded second son Fyodor Ivanovich. He was crowned Fyodor I *the Bellringer*, Tsar and Autocrat of All Russia in 1534, was supported by a five member regency council chosen by his father to help him rule. He was a simple devout man who had little interest in politics. Unfortunately the council produced a power struggle between Ivan Shuisky and Boris Godunov which was not resolved until 1587 when the Tsar's maternal uncle Godunov was the remaining member of the council.

After Fyodor I died childless, Godunov seized the throne and the title of Tsar was agreed by the *Zemsky Sobor* (National Assembly) in 1598.

Ming Dynasty China 1368-1619

Zhu Yuanzhang named his dynasty *Ming* (Brilliant) following the previous Mongol Yuan Dynasty example of taking an uplifting name. Zhu took the name Hongwu (vastly martial) as his reign-title in the capital Nanking. He tried to restore the Chinese model of empire and used the T'ang Dynasty (618-907) as an example for his government. His initial moves were to benefit the peasants by resettlement to bring fallow land under cultivation. This led to increased agricultural production and population. Hongwu's conservative communist vision was unworkable in a society that had become commercialised and mobile during the Yuan regime. Self-managed taxation by illiterate peasants was never going to work, and it was not long before bureaucrats gained power at the expense of peasants' land. After Hongwu had restored the bureaucrat examination system in 1382 the preparations for taking the examination had become quite expensive. Entry into the bureaucracy thus became restricted to the wealthy. A common speech developed based on the dialects of the North China Plain around the capital, which had grown from the late T'ang Dynasty through the Yuan Dynasty into Old Mandarin (language of officials). This developed into the twentieth century official language of China.

Hongwu died in 1398 to be succeeded by his chosen grandson Zhu Yunwen who chose the reign name Jianwen. Jianwen was challenged by his uncle, Zhu Di, the Prince of Yan, based in Beijing. Zhu Di marched with a battle-hardened army to Nanjing to successfully defeat his nephew and gain the throne in 1402 as Yung lo (Yong le). The Emperor was very careful in his search for scholars to join his government. These were not necessarily Confucianist because Yung lo was also concerned about the degeneration of Buddhism in China. Yung lo had already created a eunuch bodyguard which served him well in Beijing, with duties far from the traditional role of simply guarding the concubines. Yung lo's eunuchs were generals in the army and became a political force during his reign. His trusted eunuch Zheng He was given the task of building a fleet of vessels capable of travelling the world. Yung Lo' scholars were set to work on a project, *Yong-le-Dadian*, to preserve all known literature and knowledge. A massive encyclopaedia of around 4000 volumes was produced by 1421. A rise in tax revenues, necessary to fund Yung lo's expansive building projects at Beijing, strained the limits of the economy. Yung lo took his already assembled huge army into Mongolia to quell a possible rebellion. He died, possibly of stroke in 1424.

The mandarin aristocracy had never approved of the naval expansion and, when Zhu Gaozhi attained the throne as Emperor Hongxi, orders were given to cease shipbuilding and marine repairs. Hongxi died in 1425 to be succeeded by his son Zhu Zhanji as Emperor Xuande who admired the expansive policies of his grandfather Yung lo. Eunuchs again became more influential. Xuande ordered

Zheng He to make another world voyage in 1433 during which Zheng He died. The Ming administration was reformed and taxation regulations overhauled. Xuande recognised the independence of Vietnam in 1428 and expanded relations with Japan and Korea. The Ming Empire possibly reached a peak under Xuande.

Xuande died in 1435 to be succeeded by his eight year-old son Zhu Qizhen as Emperor Zhentong controlled by the eunuch Wang Zhen. Zhentong was captured by the Mongols but released when his brother claimed the throne as Jingtai. Zhentong regained the throne by coup in 1457 and took on a new throne name, Tianshun until his death in 1464. Under Zhu Jianshen, who ruled as Emperor Chenghua (1464-1487), the eunuchs, under Wang Zhi, increased their hold on government affairs and corruption.

Zhu Youcheng, as Emperor Hongzhi (1487-1505), had been a diligent Confucian student who took charge of his government under Confucian ideology. The Confucian bureaucrats gained control over the eunuchs, under the intelligent emperor. The isolated Chinese economy thrived under the governance of Hongzhi, largely from the natural economic growth of village industry. Unfortunately the landlord families, from whom most of the bureaucrats were drawn, had gradually expanded control of expanded landholdings.

Unfortunately Hongzhi's son, Zhu Houzhao, as Emperor Zhengde (1505-1521), was a bisexual playboy who had no real interest in ruling. Corrupt eunuchs were allowed to control government. Zhengde died childless after falling into the Grand Canal drunk. The Portuguese had reached Canton in 1516 but their attempts to establish themselves failed. They were finally allowed to settle in the island of Macao in 1557 which became their trade base for China and East Asia. A cousin, Zhu Houcong, was chosen as Emperor Jiajing (1521-1567), which sparked a Great Rites Controversy when he insisted on having his father made emperor posthumously. Jiajing was a Taoist recluse who relied totally on his minister Yah Song and his son to control government. Jiajing died in 1567, possibly of mercury poisoning, to be succeeded by his reformist son, Zhu Zaihou as Emperor Longqing (1567-1572). Longqing purged the government of corrupt officials and re-employed many talented officials who had fallen foul of his father's ministers.

Longqing' son Zhu Yijun rule as Emperor Wanli was the longest of the Ming Dynasty at 48 years. The statesman Zhang Juzheng was effectively regent for the boy (aged nine) emperor from 1572 and produced a stable government which allowed prosperity. On Zhang's death in 1582, the nineteen year-old Wanli assumed full control but reversed much of Zhang's administration. The economy was so prosperous that Wanli could not do too much damage as he attended to affairs of state. The main problems were external, particularly the invasion of Korea by Japan. In 1596 the Japanese invaded Korea again but the combined Korean and Chinese forces managed to resist. Wanli had lost interest in government which had suffered from the costs of the Korean campaigns.

Ming Emperor Wanli died in 1620 allowing his son to inherit the mess as Emperor Taichang but he was short-lived. His fifteen year-old son Zhu Youxiao succeeded as Emperor Tianqi in 1620 under the power of the Head Eunuch Wei Zhongxian and the nanny Madame Ke. Tianqi was succeeded by his younger brother Zhu Youjian who ruled as Emperor Chongzhen who immediately eliminated his brother's powerful servants. By this time the Ming Empire had deteriorated too far to be able to attract capable ministers. The Ming Empire was overtaken by the Manchu.

The Habsburg Dynasty European Empire 1477-1660

The Spanish kingdoms of Castile and Aragon were united with the 1469 marriage of Isabella and Ferdinand. In 1496 Philip *the Handsome* of Habsburg, son of the Holy Roman Emperor, married Juana, the eldest daughter of Ferdinand of Aragon and Isabella of Castile. In 1500 Juana was the clear heiress to the crowns of Aragon and Castile and was accepted as such by the *Cortes* of Castile in 1502. Philip became Felipe I of Castile in 1506 five months before his death by typhoid fever.

When Ferdinand died in 1516, the crowns of Spain (Castile as regent for his mother Juana) passed to the son of Felipe I of Castile, Karl, the Habsburg prince, as Carlos I. The Catholic Habsburgs, with Spanish power and wealth, controlled much of Europe under King Carlos of Spain/Holy Emperor Karl V. The battles over religion and the Netherlands called for large armies which led to huge debt. The first bullion from Peru had arrived in 1533 but the government's share was still only 20%, compared to 10% from that of New Spain which had commenced in 1506. In Spain, where the impact of American treasure was comparatively large, the pace of inflation actually lagged behind other parts of Europe. The Spanish government kept going by mortgaging its annual treasure fleet before the ships arrived, to foreign bankers at ruinous rates of interest. By 1543 a large part of Castilian revenue simply went to pay the interest on a public debt that was soaring out of control

The problems of a indebted government might have been a reason for Carlos' abdication in 1556 to leave Spain to his son, Felipe II, and the Holy Roman Empire to his brother Ferdinand. The loss of the 1588 Spanish Armada invasion of England was devastating to Felipe II. Felipe never raised enough cash to cover his expenditure and as a result had to declare state bankruptcies' in 1557, 1560, 1576 and 1596. The monetary problems did not improve so that the Habsburg monarchs of Spain fought a losing battle until Carlos II died childless in 1700. The succeeding French House of Bourbon did not solve the problems.

Holy Emperor Ferdinand I ruled the Habsburg House of Austria but split the hereditary lands between his three sons – Maximilian, Lower Austria; Ferdinand of Styria, Tyrol and Further Austria; and Karl, Inner Austria. The Habsburgs were plagued by wars against Protestantism and the Ottoman Empire. The independence of the Netherlands, Switzerland, Savoy, Milan, Genoa, Mantua, Tuscany, Lucca, Modena, Parma and the city of Bremen, was recognised in 1648 after the Thirty Years War. The Empire never recovered. The Habsburg rulers were not strong enough to prevent change.

The Ottoman Dynasty of Turkey 1413-1730

Sultan Murad II first attempted to breach the land walls of Byzantium (Constantinople) with light cannon in 1422. Believing peace was secure, Murad II stood down in 1430 from the throne in favour of his twelve year-old son Mehmed II. When Venice blockaded the Hellespont, Murad II came back to command the army and secured a great victory at Varna in 1444. Mehmed II prepared to conquer Byzantium as a new *ghaza* (crusade) against the source of Christian crusades against Muslim forces. The last medieval siege of Byzantium by the Turks was successful in 1453 due to the simultaneous use of the fleet and a huge land army with tremendous cannons. The city was then named *Kostantiniyye*, which Mehmed II built into the imperial political and economic centre. Mehmed II *Fatih* (Conqueror) died in 1481 before he could complete his domination of the Mediterranean. He had established the Ottomans as a power that could threaten any European nation.

Under Bayezid II, the Ottomans built a powerful navy. Europe was shocked when the Ottoman navy captured Lepanto in 1499. Sultan Selim I *Yavuz* (the Grim) led his forces into Asia Minor down the Euphrates valley which threatened the Mamluks of Egypt. Mamluk forces were soundly defeated near Aleppo so that Egypt and Syria became part of the Ottoman Empire.

The Muslim protector Sultan Suleiman *Kanuni* (the Lawgiver) was approached in 1526 by the French ambassador to rescue the Catholic king Francis I from capture in Madrid under the Habsburgs. Ottoman politics first required an attack on Hungary which was successfully invaded in 1526. Francis then encouraged the Ottomans to invade Italy but a pro-Habsburg revolt in Hungary demanded the Sultan's attention. Suleiman then had to campaign in Persia, where war had become inevitable after a revolt by pro-Habsburg forces. He left his admiral *Barbarossa* in command of all Ottoman naval forces, and provided Francis with a large gold tribute to form a coalition with England and the German princes to engage Holy Emperor Karl V. Suleiman took Baghdad from the Persians in 1535 which gave him control of Mesopotamia and naval access to the Persian Gulf. Suleiman spoke six languages and was a patron of the arts. His rule as *Padishah-i-Islam* was probably the apogee of the Ottoman Empire.

Selim II *the Sot* had none of his father's attributes and abandoned power to his ministers. Turkish naval domination of the Mediterranean finished with the Battle of Lepanto in 1571 when the Turkish fleet was annihilated. The protector of Islam and the Greek Orthodox Church was favourable to Protestantism which was considered more tolerant than Catholicism. This led to an alliance with Queen Elizabeth I of England against Catholic Habsburg hegemony in Europe. The alliance was not only political, because trade concessions to the English and Dutch merchants greatly assisted their home economies. Selim's son, Murad III, commenced his reign by having his nineteen younger brothers/half-brothers strangled. He was an idle ruler, leaving government to his mother *Safiye* Sultan. A financial crisis developed around 1580 from the influx of American silver into Empire. Currency depreciated and prices rose. The treasury moved to deficit despite increased taxes. Coincidentally the Ottomans fell behind the Europeans in military technology. Without a forceful leader there was no innovation that had initially been responsible for the rise of the Ottoman Empire. The Ottomans had stretched resources over large territories which fragmented their power.

As also happened many times in history, Persia proved the troublesome source of imperial decline. As well, despite a great victory in 1596 by the army under personal command of Sultan Mehmed III, the Austrians refused to make peace. An Anatolian revolt and shortage of money weakened Ottoman forces so that the Austrians clawed back territory. The Ottoman army had depended on Janissaries and increasing numbers of provincial irregulars, both of which were equipped with firearms and drew regular pay. The irregulars did not have full allegiance to the sultan and often withdrew before a campaign was completed.

The murder of Sultan Osman II in 1622 had resulted in the domination of imperial slaves which led to a popular rebellion. Osman's uncle Mustafa I was brought back but his inability to rule led to his deposition by Osman's younger brother Murad IV in 1623. Under virtual control of Murad's mother, the state fell into anarchy. It was not until 1635 that Sultan Murad IV imposed order and was able to lead his army against Persia. After some success a peace was obtained in 1639 which allowed the Ottomans to keep Baghdad, but renounce all claims to Azerbaijan. Ibrahim I *the Deranged* under the effective regency of his mother almost brought the Ottoman Empire to collapse.

Ibrahim I was deposed and strangled in a coup in 1648 led by Sheikh ul-Islam who installed Ibrahim's six year-old son as Mehmed IV. The Grand Vizier Mehmed Koprulu and his son rebuilt the power of the administration by fighting corruption and reorganising the Ottoman army. The Ottoman army was a shadow of its former self when Vienna was besieged in 1683. They were beaten by the combined forces of Austria, Germany and Poland. The Austrian war was not finished until 1699 and the drain on resources had placed the Ottoman Empire into a decline from which it would never recover. Rearguard action would allow the Empire to exist until the twentieth century but never as an aggressive power.

The Persian Safavid Dynasty 1501-1722

Shah Isma'il *the Great Sufi* commenced the Safavid Dynasty of Persia in 1501 when he took control of Uzbek Azerbaijan from its capital Tabriz. The core of Isma'il's army was his Qizilbash followers, Turkish warriors who shared his Shi'a religious beliefs. Shah Isma'il's first action was to proclaim the religion of his state as Shi'a Islam and enforce that religion on all subjects. Believers from the Safavid theocratic state then tried to forcibly spread Shi'a beliefs into the Sunni Ottoman Empire. The outbreak of war with the Ottomans occurred in 1514. The Safavid cavalry were no match for Ottoman mortars and muskets, and Sultan Selim occupied Tabriz.

Tahmasp I assumed leadership of the country in 1533. In 1534 Ottoman Sultan Suleiman invaded Persia with an overwhelming force. Tahmasp avoided direct contact with the large forces, but withdrew and harassed. His burned-earth policy is thought to have caused such losses that Suleiman abandoned the campaign. During the 1553 Ottoman invasion, Tahmasp captured one of Suleiman's favourites, Sinan Beg, which led to the Peace of Amasya in 1555. Never-the-less, Tahmasp withdrew his capital further from the border from Tabriz to Qazvin. Tahmasp's campaigns in the Caucasus captured many Armenians, Georgians and Circassians who were absorbed into Iran's society.

After Tahmasp's death in 1576, fighting broke out among the factions. One son was killed and, with Qizilbash support, Shah Isma'il II emerged triumphant after having been held in prison by his father for twenty years. The Qizilbash regretted their actions after Isma'il began executing supporters and princes to safeguard his throne. Isma'il himself was assassinated in 1577.

Tahmasp's son Mohammed Khodabanda had not been considered as a regal candidate when his father died because of his extremely poor eyesight, however the Qizilbash army factions chose Shah Mohammed mainly because he was last man standing. He was an amenable man whose loose rule encouraged infighting between the army and the court factions. This allowed loss of territory, including the city of Tabriz, to the Ottomans. The Shah's wife, Dhe, began to plot for the rise of her eldest son, Hamza Mirza, which brought her into conflict with the Qizilbash. Dhe was strangled in 1579. Her eldest son was murdered in 1586. When the Uzbek's invaded Khorastan in 1587, a Qizilbash leader, Murshid Qoli Khan, dethroned Mohammed and elevated Khodabanda's sixteen year-old son Abbas Mirza to the throne.

Shah Abbas I had to re-establish order in Persia, so it was necessary to negotiate a peace treaty with the Ottomans. Abbas reorganised the Persian state, commencing with an army corps of Georgian, Circassian and Armenian *ghulams* (slaves) in a similar manner to the Ottoman janissaries. By appointing Georgian *ghulam* governors, Abbas changed the administrative system away from Turk, Persian and Turcoman tribal chiefs and reduced Qizilbash influence. He also executed a number of potential tribal troublemakers. Abbas moved governors at frequent intervals so that none could gain a power-base. In 1598 Abbas moved the capital from Qazvin to Isfahan before he was able to attack the Uzbeks with his reformed army. Persian territory was cleared of Ottoman military by 1618. Baghdad was retaken by 1625. Although a Shi'ite Muslim, Abbas was tolerant of Christianity. Abbas allowed the revival of Persian culture which then flowed to Ottoman and Mughal courts. The Armenians developed a profitable trade in silks and textiles so the grateful Shah Abbas built them a Christian cathedral. He often treated Sunni Muslims harshly. Abbas showed some reverence for Sufi ancestors but his weakening of the Qizilbash led to opposition by Nuqtavi Sufis which were harshly disintegrated. Jews were persecuted. Shi'ism was dominant and the Shi'a *ulema* (council of Shi'a wise men) encouraged a School of Isfahan on Shi'a Sufism.

Abbas tried to reduce succession problems by following Ottoman practice in having his sons imprisoned in the harem. Unfortunately his paranoia led him to blind his sons, and even kill one. With no sons to succeed, Abbas was forced to choose his grandson Sam Mirza, who hated his grandfather because of the death of his father. Eighteen year-old Sam Mirza came to the throne as Shah Safi on the death of Abbas I in 1629. Shah Safi I commenced his rule by eliminating anyone who was a threat to his power, but then paid little attention to government. Safi was attracted to alcohol which some say was a major cause of his death at thirty-one in 1642.

The grand vizier Saru Taqi was regent for Safi's young son, Shah Abbas II until the vizier was assassinated in 1645 by army officers. The new vizier, Khalifa Sultan, became regent until Abbas II came of age c.1657. Abbas II enjoyed peace without Ottoman interference but did act as a warrior when Kandahar, lost by his father, was regained from the Mughals in 1648. The grand vizier, Saru Taqi, was the true ruler who kept the economy strong. In the Middle East at this time, any perceived military weakness was exploited, so that without a strong king, the Ottomans were attracted to Persian territory. Baghdad was lost to Persia in 1638 and maintained by the Ottomans until the twentieth century. The Uzbeks and Turkmens caused trouble in the east. Alcohol had been a problem with some Safavid shahs who followed Qizilbash Turko/Mongol warrior drinking culture rather than Muslim prohibition. Despite his lack of warrior activity, Shah Safi was attracted to alcohol which was a factor in his early death in 1666.

Abbas II eldest son Suleiman, who came to the throne as Shah Safi II, was brought up in the harem where alcohol must have flowed freely. He had little interest in government and a series of natural disasters caused court astrologers to suggest a new coronation at a more propitious time. In 1667 he was recrowned Suleiman I but did not change his indolent ways. He left political decision-making to his grand viziers or to a council of harem eunuchs, whose power increased during the shah's reign. Without strong control of bureaucrats, corruption became widespread and army discipline suffered. Religious power filled the court vacuum as a leading cleric, Baqer Majlesi, pushed for discrimination against non Shi'a peoples. Suleiman was lucky that the Ottomans had troubles in Europe, but the Uzbeks once again commenced raids. Alcohol is thought to have been a factor in Suleiman's death in 1694.

The court eunuchs chose the next king as the son most likely to rule peacefully. Shah Sultan Husayn was a devout Muslim so the Sufi orders were attacked and legislation introduced proscribing alcohol and opium. Such proscription was not meant for the king, and Husayn's consumption in the harem increased under the influence of his great aunt Maryam Begum. This was the time when restrictions against behaviour of Islamic women were introduced to Persia.

The long period of indolent kings resulted in a series of revolts against the regime, particularly by the Afghans and Sunni Muslims. The Afghans under Mahmud Hotaki besieged Isfahan in 1722 which submitted after six months. It is indicative of the then military weakness that the siege could not be lifted by provincial forces. Shah Sultan Husayn abdicated in 1722 to allow the Sunni Muslim, Mahmud Hotaki, to assume rule of Persia. The ruling dynasty of the Safavids had ended.

Valois/Bourbon Kings of France 1415-1793

The period under review commenced with the Burgundy-Armagnac civil war which was out of the control of the often insane Valois King Charles VI. At the time Burgundy was at least as powerful as the kingdom of France and Bernard VII, Count of Armagnac, was Constable of France who supported the king's brother Louis, Duc d'Orleans with Gascon troops. Paris erupted in revolution led by the *Cabochien* butchers. This was the tail end of the Hundred Years War so England appeared as an ally to Burgundy on the age-old principle that the *enemy of my enemy is my friend*. England won the Battle of Agincourt in 1415 and captured Paris in 1419.

After the deaths of French King Charles VI in October 1422 and English King Henry V in August 1422, the Hundred Years War stalled with the English still in control of northern France. In 1429 the teenage *Maid of Orleans*, Jeanne d'Arc, appeared to assist the Dauphin to lift the siege of Orleans and inspire the Dauphin to claim the French throne. The heroine met an unfortunate death by fire at the hands of the English, abandoned by Charles, but she had changed the course of the war. The English infant Henry VI had been acknowledged in Paris as King of France in 1422 although he was not crowned until 1431, in response to the coronation in Rheims of *de jure* King Charles VII.

In 1444 Charles VII introduced professional cavalry and artillery to create the first permanent standing army in Europe since the fall of Rome. To support this force the Estates-General voted permanent subsidies *extraordinaire des guerres*. The permanent taxes were the salt-tax (*gabelle*), property tax (*taille*) and consumer tax (*aides*). In 1453 a truce was called with England after the Battle of Castillon when France regained Aquitaine. France had been constrained from any dominance in Europe while the Hundred Years War against England continued. The kingdom was now too large for a single *parlement* so in 1454 Charles created *parlements* in the provinces to hear appeals. A body of civil servants was created that were similarly decentralised.

The Dauphin Louis demanded power from his father Charles VII and, when it was not forthcoming, stirred revolts against Charles. In 1446 Louis was banished to his province of Dauphiné, never to meet his father again despite the long illness before Charles' death in 1461. Charles VII left France relatively united for the first time since the Carolingians. His son Louis XI was a merciless monarch whose machinations gained him the appellation the Spider King (*l'universelle araignée*). He was however one of the most successful kings of France in terms of uniting his country. He fostered trade and manufacturing in the cities which increased the economy and of course royal taxes. He brought the power of the cities to the fore in his battle to depower the nobility.

Charles VIII was one of a number of French monarchs that came to power under the regency of their mother and who were not strong rulers. The thirteen year-old Charles VIII (*l'affable*), under the regency of Louis' daughter, Anne de Beaujeu, became betrothed to Margaret of Austria who would bring Habsburg Burgundy to France as her dowry. In 1490 Charles VIII had to renounce Margaret in order to marry Anne of Brittany to obtain the great Celtic duchy of Brittany for France. The long term animosity between French royalty and the Habsburgs commenced. Charles came of age in 1491.

Charles VIII was enticed to Italy in 1493 by the Duc de Milan to claim Naples. This commenced French royal participation in Italian wars that were to last nearly a 100 years. The first opposition to the French was the League of Venice formed by Pope Alexander VI (Borgia), King Ferdinand of Aragon, Holy Emperor Maximilian and the Duke of Milan (whose daughter had married Maximilian). The League forces were not as commanding as the titles of their patrons, and the French managed to rout them to recross the Alps albeit with the loss of booty and equipment.

When Charles VIII died childless in a household accident in 1498 he was succeeded by Louis, Duc d'Orleans as Louis XII *Père du Peuple*. Saddled with debt from Charles' Italian adventures, Louis XII reformed government and reduced taxes. When debt was under control, Louis invaded Milan to which he claimed title through his grandmother, but also to discipline Ludovico Sforza. Ferdinand of Aragon offered to share Naples so French troops moved to govern their territory. There was a dispute over ill-defined borders which resulted in battles against Spanish troops. The Spanish won and the French retreated to Naples.

The *Warrior Pope*, Julius II, formed the League of Cambrai in 1508 with Louis XII, Maximilian and Ferdinand, largely to retake Venetian advances. The League was largely unsuccessful and it broke up, when France withdrew in 1510. The Holy League of 1511 was formed with Aragon, Empire and England. The French retreated over the Alps not the least because the League partners threatened France itself. Ferdinand attacked the south and English Henry VIII landed troops in Calais. After the death of Julius, who had been inciting the foment, a truce was signed in 1514 which was sealed with the marriage of Louis to Mary Tudor. The 16 year-old Mary might have been too much for the 52 year-old Louis, who lived only three months after the marriage.

The childless Louis was succeeded by his nephew Francis of Angouleme who became Francis I at twenty-one. He invaded Italy and was victorious against a Swiss mercenary army to recapture Milan. In 1517 Francis founded the French port of Le Havre. The maritime interest was continued later in the reign with assistance to found trading posts in the Americas, including Newfoundland, New Angouleme (New York) and Quebec. The deaths occurred of Habsburg Ferdinand (1516) and Maximilian (1519) who were succeeded by Maximilian's son Karl, who outbribed Francis in the election for Holy Roman Emperor. The spread of Protestantism occupied much of Karl's time but he was determined to reclaim Burgundy and to oust Francis from Italy. Francis I became one of the great kings of France although his egotistic battles with Emperor Karl V were very costly. He formed the policy of cooperating with the enemies of his Hamburg enemy such as the Ottoman Empire. After the Peace of the Ladies in 1530, Francis married Eleanor, the sister of Karl V in 1537. Francis declared French the national language of the kingdom and downgraded Latin. The troublesome reign of Francis came to an end in 1547, leaving an economically and religiously troubled France to his remaining son as Henri II.

Henri II continued his father's anti-Protestant policy in the wars against the Huguenots as well as fighting Karl V. The alliances of Francis I with the Protestant princes of Germany and the infidel Ottoman Empire were continued.

The Habsburg-Valois War of 1551-1559 occurred when Henri declared war on Karl V with the intention of regaining Italian territory for France. In 1552 Maurice of Saxony led Protestant forces against Karl who was forced to flee to the Netherlands. The attempted French invasion of Tuscany in 1553 was defeated at the Battle of Marciano. Wars continued with the Habsburgs, firstly in Flanders in 1557 which resulted in a loss to the French. Henri countered by capturing Calais and savaging the Netherlands. In the Peace of Cateau-Cambresis (1559) Henri agreed to renounce any claims to Italy. In the joust celebrating the Peace, Henri was mortally wounded and succeeded by his son Francis II under the regency of Queen Catherine.

Francis II was a fifteen year-old inept teenager when he gained the throne a year after he had married Marie Stuart who had been raised in the French court. Francis was dominated by the seventeen year-old Marie in bed and in court. Marie's uncle, Francois de Guise became supreme in the royal council, although unpopular with other nobles. Francis II became dominated by the Catholic de Guise family so the religious wars continued. Francis II died, possibly of a brain abscess in 1560. Marie returned to Scotland in 1561 to enter history in another guise (Mary Queen of Scots).

The Queen Mother Catherine de Medici was regent to ten year-old Charles-Maximilian who ruled as Charles IX. Charles IX had to suffer the formal French Religious Wars in 1562, 1567, 1568 and 1572. The Atlantic ports became havens for Dutch and English privateers and pirates who attacked Spanish and Portuguese shipping. When Catholic pickings were slim, privateers became pirates who attacked Protestant shipping to and from England. Charles IX died in 1574, to leave the throne to his brother Alexandre, already King of Poland and Grand Duc de Lithuania, and who ruled France as Henri III.

Henri III was immediately involved in the next religious wars in 1575 and 1577. The Treaty of Monsieur in 1576 favoured the Protestants because Henri III did not have the money to pay his own troops. The Catholic League of the Duc de Guise operated as a state within a state and acted independently from the king to spark civil war called the War of the Henri's. When outside threats had been neutralised by the English defeat of the Spanish Armada, Henri III called a meeting of Estates-General but the Duc de Guise had them baying for Protestant blood. In defence, Henri III had the popular Henri de Guise murdered by his guards in 1588. The Guises raised troops and proclaimed Charles, Cardinal de Bourbon, king as Charles X. The Pope excommunicated Henri III. The Catholic

Parlement charged Henri III with murder so he joined forces with Henri de Navarre to recapture Paris and the north under the auspices of the *Parlement de Tours*. A Dominican fanatic was used to assassinate Henri III in 1589 and the attack on Paris faded away

Henri de Navarre was nominally King of France, supported by England but had to win his kingdom from the Catholic League and Spain. Henri chose to renounce Protestantism to attract the allegiance of his subjects. He was crowned Henri IV of France in 1594 as first of the Bourbon dynasty. After he was recommunicated in 1595, Henri worked for reconciliation of the two religious faiths and managed a peace after the Edict of Nantes in 1598. During his reign, Henri IV worked through his steadfast minister Maximilien de Béthune, Duc de Sully, to regularise state finance, promote agriculture, drain swamps to create productive crop lands, undertake many public works, and encourage education. Unfortunately the Treasury was in such a parlous state on Sully's arrival, that financial progress was slow. He paid off much of the public debt by devaluing the currency by a third. Henri IV was a popular king who stemmed the fall of France into religious anarchy, but was unable to stimulate the country into a further rise in greatness. Another religious fanatic assassinated Henry IV in 1610.

Queen Mother Maria de Medici was regent for the nine year-old Louis XIII. At the meeting of the Estates in 1614 Maria introduced Armand du Plessis de Richelieu into the Council of State. During the Thirty Years War, Cardinal Richelieu as Chief Minister had the policy to centralise power; to ruin the Huguenots, to shake the pretensions of the great nobles and to humble the power of Austria. Richelieu's power attracted an unsuccessful revolution from the nobles under Louis' younger brother Duc d'Orleans. Richelieu raised the salt-tax (*gabelle*) and land tax (*taille*) to relieve the strain on France's finance. He made a pre-emptive strike against Spain which was unsuccessful but lasted ten years. Richelieu was instrumental in redirecting the Thirty Years' War from the conflict of Protestantism versus Catholicism, to that of nationalism versus Habsburg hegemony. Before his death in 1642, the dying Cardinal, Duc de Richelieu, named his follower, the Jesuit, Jules Cardinal Mazarin as successor. Louis XIII *the Just* had been ill for some time and was carried on a litter. He died in 1643 just before French victory against the Spanish at Rocroi which took away the myth of Spanish military invincibility.

Anne of Austria became Regent for five year-old Louis XIV but in fact power resided in Mazarin. The French victory at Rocroi gave rise to four years of negotiations which resulted in a favourable treaty in 1648 after another victory for the French at Lens. France's external strength was magnified by the German fragmentation after the Peace of Westphalia. Alsace was added to French territory. Taxes had to be increased which *Parlement de Paris* refused, even after Mazarin imprisoned the Duc de Beaufort. Mazarin tried again to re-establish the war tax, "*Paulette*" but *Parlement* rose against him. Taxes were not the only problem because Mazarin had been attacking privileges of the feudal aristocracy. Following the imprisonment of a *Parlement* leader, Pierre Broussel, Paris revolted. Mazarin and the Queen Mother Anne made an edict to exile the leaders of state to the provinces. The leaders declared Mazarin an enemy of the state. Mazarin had Louis de Bourbon, Prince de Condé, and his brother Armand, Prince de Conti, arrested, which provoked regional unrest. Anne was forced to release the Princes and Mazarin fled the country. Civil war broke out with *Parlement's* army led by the general, Prince de Condé, besieging Paris. The royal court fled. The rebels started to negotiate with Spain which led Parlement to separate itself from the rebellion, known as *Fronde Parlementaire*. Mazarin returned with an army but troops of the *Fronde* besieged Paris. Mazarin left again and Louis, who had come of age to rule, promised an amnesty. Paris was recaptured.

Louis XIV was crowned in 1654 and confirmed Mazarin's power as a virtual dictator along the same lines as Richelieu. Mazarin allied France with the England's Protestant Protector Cromwell, who put the English navy at France's disposal against Spain. The conflict was ended by the Peace of the Pyrenees in 1659 which added Roussillon, Artois and French Cerdanya to French territory. Cromwell had been promised Dunkirk, but had died so the promise was not kept.

Mazarin died in 1661and Louis declared that he would rule without a first minister. The Treasury verged on bankruptcy when Louis assumed the throne, so Louis chose Jean-Baptiste Colbert as *Controleur General des Finances* in 1665. Colbert reduced the national debt through more efficient taxation, and bolstered France's commerce and trade. However, he handled the public debt by repudiating bonds and ruining bondholders which would make future debt difficult. Colbert encouraged immigration of skilled artisans to build up manufacturing so as to reduce imports and increase exports. *Le Grande Ordonnance de Procédure Civile* of 1667, also known as *Code Louis*, was a comprehensive legal code attempting a uniform regulation of civil procedure throughout legally irregular France. The army was modernised into a professional, disciplined and well trained force with less influence by individual nobles.

The haughty Louis XIV, who is reputed to have made the statement *"L'etat c'est moi"*, was equally imperious with Europe so that, at one time or another, he attracted enmity of the Empire, Holy See, Turkey and England. In 1667 France overran the Spanish Netherlands following the death of Felipe IV, on the basis that the promised dowry of his wife had not been paid. Spain sought alliances of the United Provinces and the Empire. The United Provinces were happy to have the Spanish Netherlands as a buffer against France and offered to mediate. When Louis was examining the idea of war against the Dutch, they tried to get an alliance together against France. They succeeded in 1668 with the Triple Alliance of England, Sweden and the United Provinces. A peace treaty to end the War of Devolution was negotiated which left twelve cities, including Lille and Tournai, in French hands. The Queen's rights to Spanish Succession were recognised.

The French Secretary of State for War, Marquis de Louvois, prepared for war by reorganising the army and increasing its strength. Thus fortified in 1672, Louis declared war on the United Provinces. De Witt, who had organised that alliance against Louis, was lynched and William III of Nassau was made *stadtholder*. In response to a French extortion threat, the Dutch inundated the land to stop further French advance. The Dutch then stopped a sea invasion by defeating the Anglo-French fleet. England abandoned the war in 1674. The Dutch attracted allies from the Empire and Spain, and the Franco-Dutch War ended with the Treaty of Nijmegen in 1678. Louis kept Franche-Comte and a number of cities at the expense of Spain.

Louis XIV annexed Strasbourg in 1682 in the year that he moved into the fabulously expensive *Chateau de Versailles*. In 1683 Louis revoked the Edict of Nantes with that of Fontainebleau which instituted forced baptism of Protestants and demolished churches. Louis moved to expel Protestants from France. The mass exodus from France stripped the country of many skills and forced those remaining Protestants to worship clandestinely. Clandestine Protestantism became a political faction. Maybe 1% of the French population, including many of the elite, fled religious persecution. Also in 1683 Spain declared war over the attempts by France to annex Luxembourg. Spanish forces were no match for the French, and the war was over by 1684. The conflict did not solve festering French feelings against the Habsburgs. France had gained a reputation for arrogance and brutality. The French persecutions provoked the German Protestant princes who united in 1686 in the League of Augsburg, which brought together the Elector of Brandenburg, the Emperor, Venice, Russia, Poland, Spain, Sweden, Bavaria and Holland. While negotiations dragged on, Louis took pre-emptive action by occupying a number of German cities. A revolution in England installed William III of Orange who took England into the League.

The War of the Augsburg League started in 1689 with French victories from Flanders in the north, Germany in the east, Italy and Spain in the south to the high seas and the colonies. Then allied victories started to appear which made both sides ready to negotiate a peace. The war finished with the Treaty of Ryswick in 1697 in which France gave back some of its gains but kept Alsace, including Strasbourg. The War of Spanish Succession commenced when Louis sent troops into the Spanish Netherlands. He evicted Dutch troops from the "barrier" and secured Dutch acceptance of Felipe V.

Louis took no notice of the parlous state of French finances. The Emperor formed another Grand Alliance with German petty states, England, and the United Provinces. The arrogant Louis had allies Portugal, Bavaria, and Savoy. The first three years of the War of Spanish Succession saw French victories under Marshalls Berwick and Villars against the allies under Prince Eugene of Savoy. The victory of General Marlborough and Eugene of Savoy at Blenheim in 1704, caused Bavaria to be occupied, and a switch to the allies of Portugal and Savoy. After victory at Velez-Malaga, the English occupied Gibraltar, which was used as a base to blockade the French navy. From 1706 onwards the Franco-Spanish forces fought a defensive retreat which lost the Netherlands and Lille. In 1709 Prince Eugene besieged Landrecies which guarded the road to Paris. In 1714 the Empire also made peace with France in the Treaty of Rastadt. Felipe V retained Spain and the colonies; Austria received the Low Countries (Belgium) and divided Spanish Italy with Savoy; Britain kept Gibraltar and Minorca, was ceded Newfoundland, Rupert's Land, and Arcadia, and gained a presence in Dunkirk; France basically kept the pre-war *status quo*.

Unfortunately France could not afford this imperious king. The financial situation of France was dire, and the melting of the last of Louis' silver could only be a stop-gap measure. Then in 1711, *le grand dauphin* died of smallpox followed in 1712 by the succeeding *dauphin*, Duc de Burgundy. The Duc de Berry died in 1714, leaving a child Louis, Duc d'Anjou, as the last legitimate heir. Louis XIV on his death bed declared that his bastards could inherit, but he died in 1715 before further royal deaths.

The regent of Louis XV led France into infamous bankruptcy in 1720, but his government under Cardinal de Fleury produced a stable period. The

Seven Years War against Britain, away from Europe, lost the French colonial empire. *Parlement* was by this time nearly permanently in revolt due to the parlous financial situation. Choiseul negotiated the marriage of the *dauphin* Louis to Marie Antoinette of Austria to consolidate the alliance. *Parlement* revolted again at moves to curb any independence. Louis responded by dismissing the body and exiling its members. The seeds for the Revolution were well and truly sown. Louis ruled by Grand Council, led by the Triumvirate of Maupeou, Terray and Aiguillon who were advocates of absolute monarchical rule. There were efforts to reduce and reform taxation but they were too little too late. Louis died of smallpox in 1774.

Louis XVI inherited the unpopularity that had soured his grandfather's last years. Determined to be a good king, Louis chose the Comte de Maurepas as first minister, Vergennes in foreign affairs and Turgot in finance. *Parlement* was re-established and Turgot tried to introduce unpopular taxation reforms. Vergennes was watching the American rebellion closely but Turgot had told him that finances prevented any war. Turgot introduced rigid economies in government and tried to reform pensions which reduced the deficit but were unpopular. The poor 1774 harvest coincided with a measure to introduce free trade in grain, which raised alarm from the nobles who speculated in grain, and caused riots by the peasants. Many of Turgot's reforms were blocked by *Parlement*. Turgot was replaced in 1776 by a Genevan banker Jacques Necker. Necker supported the American Revolution and proceeded to take large international loans instead of raising taxes. In 1778 a treaty of friendship was signed with American Benjamin Franklin. When Britain found out about the treaty, it declared war, but actions were light close to France. The French fleet went to America but was mostly unsuccessful in its encounters. In 1780 an expeditionary force under Rochambeau was sent to America but it was undermanned. In 1781 Rochambeau joined Washington's forces which were successful in Yorktown, as was the navy under Admiral de Grasse. French intervention proved decisive in forcing a British army under Lord Cornwallis to surrender in 1781.

The financial crisis as a result of the war surfaced in 1781, so Necker was sacked in 1783 to be replaced by *le Compte de* Calonne. Calonne's idea was to increase public spending to buy the country out of debt (*shades of 2008!*). Despite the financial crisis, Louis was determined to expel the British from India. Troops were moved from Mauritius. Louis XVI called an Assembly of Notables in 1787 to discuss further fiscal reform but the nobles were shocked at the extent of public debt and rejected the plan. Calonne was sacked. Lomenie de Brienne was made first minister. When he realised that he had insufficient funds to pay August dues, Brienne resigned in 1788. Necker was recalled as chief minister.

After considerable trouble with *Parlements*, a depressed Louis in 1789 was talked into calling the first Estates-General since 1614 in an attempt to get some monetary reform. After a month of fruitless discussions the Third Estate constituted themselves as the National Assembly. Louis swore an oath to give the country a constitution, and then changed his mind. He then dismissed Necker and called his troops in preparation for bankruptcy if the Estates did not vote the necessary credit. Paris was soon consumed by riots, chaos, and widespread looting. The mobs soon had the support of some of the French Guard, who were armed and trained soldiers. The insurgents set their eyes on the large weapons and ammunition cache inside the Bastille fortress, which was also perceived to be a symbol of royal power. The French Revolution was under way.

In September 1792 The French National Assembly declared France to be a Republic and abolished the monarchy. Louis was stripped of all titles to become Citizen Louis Capet. In December Louis was accused of High Treason and crimes against the State. In January 1793 the National Assembly voted overwhelmingly to find Louis guilty, but the vote for execution passed by only a slim majority. Louis XVI was executed by guillotine in January 1793.

India under the Mughal Emperors 1560-1764

The Mughal Empire was founded by Zahir-ud-din Muhammad Babur, a descendent of *Tamerlane* on his father's side and of Genghis Khan on his mother's side. As happened previously with the Mongols, many of Babur's *amirs* (nobles) disliked the heat of India and had no desire to stay. On his death in 1530 Babur was succeeded by his son Nasir ud-din Muhammad Humayun who had the task of consolidating his father's conquests.

Unfortunately the young man indulged himself in pleasure; wine and opium so that his father's hard-won gains were lost by 1540 to Sher Khan. Humayun was forced into exile in Persia. After years in Persia, Humayun gained support from the Persian Shah to raise an army to reconquer the Indian empire. In 1545 he regained Kabul and Kandahar and in 1554 set out for India. Under guidance of his general Bairam Khan, the army had two resounding victories to regain Delhi and Agra. He had brought with him around fifty *amirs* (nobles), Turkish/Uzbek and Persian. Humayun was unable to complete full conquest because he died of an accidental fall in 1556.

Abu'l-Fath Jalal-ud-Din Muhammad Akbar, guided by his father's Persian general Bairam Khan, consolidated of power in northern India. Akbar reduced the power of those who had assisted his father and replaced them with Persian *amirs* and Indian born nobles from leading Muslim families. Akbar's greatest strength was the bureaucracy necessary to govern a vast region. The young man was astute enough to realise the efficiency of Sher Khan's administration. The civil service (*mansabars*) had thirty-three grades with regular ranks and fixed salaries. Tax collection on land was an important part of empire, and Akbar imposed his tax on everyone including nobles. The tax on non-believers of Islam (*jizya*) was abolished in a move which gained much popularity from the Hindus. The bulk of the empire's revenue went directly to the *amirs* through *jagirs* (land holding revenues). The administrative language was Persian. Akbar cemented relationships in his territory by marrying daughters of kings so that he had over five thousand concubines and wives, mainly for political reasons.

In 1605 Akbar died and is now considered one of the greatest rulers of India, on a par with the Mauryan Emperor, Asoka *the Great* (273-232BC). The Timurid tradition did not recognise the rights of the eldest son to automatically succeed, so that years of intrigue often occurred before succession. Akbar's eldest surviving son Salim was in opposition to the teenage son Khusrau and Salim's third son Khurram (later Shah Jahan). Salim succeeded despite his earlier revolt and took the name Jahangir (conqueror of the world). He built on his father's administration to create political stability and a strong economy. Jahangir followed the religious tolerance of his father and some of his closest nobles and courtiers were Hindu. Prince Khurram, a brilliant military strategist, completed the main victory of Jahangir's reign. He completed the subjection of the Rahjputs by persuading Karam Sing to accept imperial rank. Sikhs were controlled and the Deccan campaigns were resumed. During his reign, Udaipur, which had resisted Mughal will, was brought into empire. Unfortunately Jahangir was not the general that his father was, and had his grandfather's self-indulgence and addictions to wine and opium. As his addictions took more hold Jahangir came fully under the influence of his wife Mehr-ul-nisa (*Nur Jahan* - light of the world) and her father chief minister (*diwan*) Itimad-ud-daulah. They intrigued to provoke several power struggles which came close to open rebellion. Nur Jahan had a bitter struggle with her step-son Prince Khurram. In 1615 the English crown requested Sir Thomas

Roe to visit Shah Jahangir to obtain a foothold in India. A treaty was arranged to allow the East India Company rights to build factories in Surat in the state of Gujarat. The Company then obtained permission to set up a fortified trading post on the Coromandel Coast in 1639. The Fort of St. George was to grow into the city of Madras (modern Chennai). The Mughals understood the value of maritime commerce and tried to keep the freedom of trade to India's coasts, but they lacked an effective navy.

Khurram attained the throne as Shah Jahan (*Tamerlane's* title - king of the world) on his father's death in 1628. He forced Nur Jahan into retirement in Agra. Relatives who might be rivals were killed. Under Jahangir and Shah Jahan the number of Persian *amirs* increased largely due to Nur Jahan's influence and the enforcement of harsh Shi'a Islam under the Safavids. Shah Jahan reformed the army by reducing the number of horses provided by *mansabdars* and by reducing pay rates of *amirs*. The numbers of *amirs* would remain a problem throughout the century. In the Deccan, Shah Jahan defeated Khan Jahan Lohdi. In the 1630s the sultanates of Golconda and Bijapur were annexed. The Deccan was twice placed under the control of Shah Jahan's third son, Aurangzeb. Shah Jahan's eldest son, the scholarly Dara Shukoh opposed the younger's aggressive actions at court, and engineered a peace.

Shah Jahan's wife, Mumtaz Mahal, died in 1630 in childbirth and he lived in mourning for two years. In 1632 he commenced building the mausoleum to his great love which took twenty-five years to finish. The Taj Mahal (officially *Rauza-i Munawwar* – Illumined Tomb) in Agra is considered Mughal India's greatest masterpiece. In 1638 Shah Jahan moved his capital to Delhi where he built a new palace in a new city Shahjahanabad which is now the walled city of Old Delhi. Near the palace Jahan built the largest mosque in India, Jami Masjid. Shah Jahan had adopted a more traditional attitude towards Islam than his predecessors. Under his rule, the empire became a huge military machine and the nobles with their contingents multiplied almost fourfold, as did the demands for more revenue from the peasantry. Due to his measures in the financial and commercial fields, it was a period of general stability—the administration was centralised and court affairs systematised. The constant pressure on the Deccan finally had results in 1636 when the kingdom of Ahmednagar fell to the Mughals.

Unfortunately the Persians took advantage of internal dissent to capture the Afghan fortress of Kandahar (*Qandahar*) in 1653 so that the Mughals lost control over the trade routes to Central Asia. Shah Jahan and his sons recaptured the city of Kandahar in 1638 from the Safavids, prompting the retaliation of the Persians led by their powerful ruler Abbas II of Persia, who recaptured it in 1649. The Mughal armies were then unable to recapture it despite repeated sieges during the Mughal–Safavid War. In 1657 Shah Jahan fell seriously ill and it was rumoured that he had died. This started a war of succession by his four sons. Aurangzeb executed Dara Shikoh and Murad, and exiled Shah Shuja. Shah Jahan recovered from his illness but was imprisoned in the palace for the rest of his life. Some historians state that the Mughals' high point occurred under Shah Jahan, but at the end he had only power to gaze mournfully in the direction of the Taj Mahal until his death in 1666. The Mughal Empire is considered to have peaked with the deposition of Shah Jahan in 1658, although the peak of Mughal territorial Empire did not occur until 1687. I am inclined to choose 1687 after which Aurangzeb's territory started to breakdown.

In 1661 English King Charles II received Indian islands as a Portuguese dowry which allowed the East India Company to move their main holdings from Surat to Bombay (Mumbai). The city developed from a simple fort into the formidable port of Bombay which became the trade and financial capital of India by the end 1700s. In 1686, the English East India Company, which had unsuccessfully tried to obtain a *firman* (imperial directive) that would grant England regular trading privileges throughout the Mughal Empire, initiated the so-called Child's War. This hostility against the empire ended in disaster for the English, particularly when Aurangzeb dispatched a strong fleet from Janjira. In 1690 the company sent envoys to Aurangzeb's camp to plead for a pardon. The English pirate Henry Every captured a Mughal convoy returning from Mecca. Aurangzeb was persuaded not to eliminate the English from Bombay, when the East India Company agreed to pay huge financial reparations.

Aurangzeb who ruled as Alamgir I (conqueror of the universe) from 1658 returned to the policy of aggressive expansion. He reasserted Mughal authority in Bengal when the governor, Mir Jumla, annexed Kuch Bihar in North Bengal and subdued most of Assam. The Nawabs of Murshidabad, who respected the nominal sovereignty of the Mughals in Delhi, granted permission to the French *Compagnie des Indes* to establish a trading post at Chandernagore in 1673. Aurangzeb abandoned the liberal religious policies introduced by Akbar. His attempts to replace the law code of Hindu law with Shari'a law incensed the Hindu population which bred rebellion. In the Punjab, the Sikhs rebelled from a peaceful religious sect to a strong hostility of Islam. The Sikhs had formed along military lines and were formidable rebels. A Pashtun revolt around the Khyber Pass in 1672 was never finally resolved and the Mughals and lost another source of warriors. In pursuing the Deccan wars, Aurangzeb alienated the Mughal nobility, whose sacrifices, in their opinion, were not sufficiently rewarded. Aurangzeb's long absence in the Deccan allowed further intransigence in the north, and growing independence of regional governors.

The Hindu Marathas were a blend of the *Kshatriya* (warrior) and agrarian peasant classes, clan based that were united in battle by Shavaji Bhonsle (1630-80) from his centre at Pune, south of Surat. After being defeated by the Mughals, in 1665 Shavaji escaped to his hill fortresses and proclaimed himself an independent ruler in 1674. The Maratha's, who waged guerrilla war in the Deccan for 27 years, intensified their campaigns in the barren mountain ranges of the Western Ghats. As the Americans later found in twentieth century Vietnam, a huge army is cumbersome and costly against mobile and active guerrilla warfare. Aurangzeb lost about a fifth of his army fighting rebellions led by the Marathas in the Deccan.

Aurangzeb's son, Muhammad Akbar rebelled to flee to Rajputana and in 1681 declared himself emperor. Akbar marched against his father with his Mughal forces allied to Rahjput cavalry and Rathore war bands. Before the forces could meet, Aurangzeb arranged false information which caused the Rahjput forces to retire and Akbar's army to retreat. Akbar joined the Marathas but the king was too busy to take on Aurangzeb directly. In 1686 Akbar moved to Persia where he died in 1704.

In 1686 the East India Company sent a fleet of ten ships to India as a show of force to the Mughals, who it was believed were putting obstacles in the way of trade out of Bombay and Bengal. The subsequent war was a failure resulting in heavy EIC indemnity. In 1690 the English established a fortified port down river from the Mughal port of Hugli in Bengal that was silting up. In 1702, the British completed the construction of old Fort William, which was used to station its troops and as a regional base. Calcutta (Kolkata), the site of Fort William, grew into the source of expensive fine fabrics for the high-end European market

After Aurangzeb's death in 1707 at age eighty-eight, his son Qutb ud-Din Muhammad Mu'azzam as Bahadur Shah I succeeded to a throne under deep pressure from his father's policies. First he had to defeat his brothers Azam Shah and Muhammad Kam Bakhsh in succession wars. He brought an end to the long running Rajput animosity by making peace. He savagely put down another Sikh revolt. By cunning diplomacy Bahadur managed to incite a Maratha civil war so that for most of his reign they fought each other. Bahadur Shah was sixty-six when he took the throne and was too old and militarily inept to do much more than shakily hold on to power. His death in 1712 sparked off the Mughal decline with another succession war.

Jahandar Shah won the succession struggle against his brother but was able to rule only eleven months. Jahandar Shah was defeated in battle in 1713 by his nephew Farrukh-siyar who had him strangled on the orders of the powerful generals, Sayyid brothers. Shah Farrukh-siyar would spend most of his reign trying to bribe notable Mughal servicemen to overthrow the Sayyid Brothers. In 1739 the Persian Emperor Nader Shah took advantage of the disarray caused by a series of short-lived rulers to invade India. Muhammad Shah's army was easily defeated so that the Persians entered Delhi within a month. He granted Muhammad Shah's pleas for mercy in exchange for the Mughal treasure, including the fabled Peacock Throne.

The Mughal Empire basically collapsed after the Persian invasion. It is said the Muhammad Shah died of shame in 1748. Mughal Shah Alam II could not contest the growing control of India by the East India Company. The Company received a coerced appointment from Shah Alam II to be the body in charge of commerce (*diwan*) for Bengal, Bihar and Orissa in 1764. A wealthy Robert Clive was appointed Governor of Bengal in 1765 when the Company took over the administration of the province. The second son of Alam II, Akbar Shah II came to the throne in 1816 but had little power. The East India Company was frustrated at his pretence as a sovereign and reduced his titular authority to "King of Delhi" in 1835 and discontinued issuing coins in his name. Akbar's son succeeded him in 1837 as Bahadur Shah Zafar but was treated as a pensioner of the Red Fort by the Company. The last Mughal Emperor was exiled to Burma by the Company for his support of the India Revolution of 1857.

The Tokugawa Shoguns of Japan 1591-1853

Japan had an emperor since 660BC but the degree of power exercised by the emperor varied considerably throughout history. The need for an army to maintain power led to powerful generals who from time to time were able to dominate the imperial government. In 797, the general Sakanoe no Tamuramaro was accorded the title *seii tai-shogun* (barbarian-suppressing supreme general) which led to domination of the emperor by the Fujiwara clan (794-1185). Private armies including mounted warriors (*saburahi- samurai*) kept the period unstable. The growth of the *samurai* class from the 10th century gradually weakened the power of the imperial family over the nation. The first general to be known as *shogun* was Minomotu no Yoritomo in 1192 who was granted the title by Emperor Go-Toba.

The provincial governors lost control in favour of more powerful *daimyo* (feudal lords) to whom *samurai* (noble warriors) swore allegiance. The *samurai* became fief holders in control of land and people, often surrounding castle-towns of their *daimyo*. As often occurs in civil wars, a strong warlord would arise to unify fighters to his own ends. Odo Nobunaga dominated central Japan to commence the shogunate that would last until 1868.

After the Battle of Okehazama 1560, Nobunaga formed an alliance with the Matsudaira clan leader, Tokugawa Ieyasu. Other clans were mostly weakened or destroyed through war during which thousands of non-combatants were killed. At the decisive Battle of Nagashino 1575, the combined forces of Nobunaga and Tokugawa Ieyasu devastated the Takeda clan with the strategic use of arquebus firearms. Nobunaga compensated for the arquebus' slow reloading time by arranging the arquebusiers in three lines. At the height of his power in 1582, Oda Nobunaga was killed through betrayal of an insulted general.

Although the son of a peasant/foot soldier, Hideyoshi rose through the ranks to become a *samurai* who adopted the surname Hashiba c.1567. At the time of Nobunaga's death, his loyal general (Hashiba) Toyotomi Hideyoshi was in control of more than half of Japanese provinces. In 1573 after victorious campaigns, Nobunaga made Hideyoshi *daimyo* of three districts in Omi Province, where he took control of Kunitomo firearms factory. In 1582 Hideyoshi defeated the general who had killed his liege lord Nobunaga, before destroying the Oda clan's chief general Shibata Katsuie in the battle for succession. As a commoner Hideyoshi could not gain the title of shogun, but was granted the title of *kampaku* (regent) by the imperial court. It was the imperial court which granted him the surname/clan Toyotomi in 1586.

Born Matsudaira Takechiyo in 1543 to the daimyo of Mikawa, Ieyasu had been a child hostage of clan warfare. In 1567 after consolidating Mikawa vassals, Ieyasu adopted the name Tokugawa Ieyasu claiming descent from the imperial Minamotu clan. He was an ally of Oda Nobunaga but actively sought non-conflicting clan alliances. On the death of Nobunaga, Ieyasu found himself in conflict with Toyotomi Hideyoshi but their war was settled by negotiation. After allying with Hideyoshi, Ieyasu reformed his provinces and grew to become the second most powerful *daimyo* in Japan. Thus Ieyasu became the most powerful of the Council of Five regents to govern until Hideyoshi's infant son came of age.

The last resistance to Hideyoshi's authority fell in 1590. Tokugawa Ieyasu was allowed control over eight provinces. He placed trading cities of Osaka and Nagasaki under his direct control to gain income from international trade. Hideyoshi was succeeded in 1590 as regent by his nephew Toyotomi Hidetsugu who was ordered to commit *seppuku* (stomach cutting suicide) in 1595. Hideyoshi then ordered the deaths of the entire Hidetsugu family, which effectively weakened the Toyotomi clan. In his declining years Hideyoshi had plans to invade China and requested that Korea allow his troops to pass on the way to China. Refusal meant war with Korea which was occupied by 1593. The Ming army provided relief to Korea. Japanese troops were withdrawn after the death of Hideyoshi in 1598.

By 1599 the *daimyos* had formed two factions – three other regents allied to Ishida Mitsunari and Honshu *daimyo* against Ieyasu and a number of eastern clans. Ieyasu was victorious at the Battle of Sekigahara 1600 to become *de facto* ruler of Japan.

In 1603 Tokugawa Ieyasu received the title of *shogun* from Emperor Go-Yozai. Ieyasu shifted *daimyo* to provinces where they were less likely to question his power. He instituted *buke-sho-hatto* (laws for military houses) which governed the life of *daimyo*, from reporting on castle improvements which the shogun needed to approve, to *daimyo* marriage. *Daimyo* were divided into groups with those close to the Tokugawa line receiving preference in official positions. The Tokugawa family and loyal vassals held 60% of Japanese land, whereas the *tozama* (outside houses) jointly held about 40%. A network of informants was established to report on activity in fiefs. Powerful regional families – Shimuzu clan, Kagoshima; Chosu *han* (territory), Honshu; Tosa *han*, Shinkoku – were treated with respect because outer regions were difficult to control. Japan had all the characteristics of a police state and a closed society.

Ieyasu abdicated the title in 1605 to allow his son Tokugawa Hidetada to act as formal head of the *bakufu* (government) at Edo (modern Tokyo). Ieyasu supervised the building of Edo Castle which became the largest castle in Japan (site of modern Imperial Palace). In 1614 as *ogosho* (retired shogun), Ieyasu signed the "Christian Expulsion Edict" which banned Christianity and expelled Christians and foreigners. Toyotomi Hideyoshi's son Hideyori attracted *daimyo* that opposed

Ieyasu at Osaka Castle. The initial siege was finished through negotiation but Hideyori refused to leave the castle. The second siege was followed by a massacre in 1615 which killed the Toyotomi clan. Ieyasu died in 1616 aged 73.

Tokugawa Hidetada strengthened the hold on power by having his daughter married to Emperor Go-Mizunoo. Edo was expanded under the reign of Hidetada who resigned in 1623 as *shogun* in favour of Tokugawa Iemitsu. Like his father, Hidetada persecuted Christians and forced Christian *daimyo* to commit suicide. Tokugawa Iemetsu was a follower of the *shudo* (homosexual) tradition and made lavish grants of money/gold to imperial court nobles. His niece, Meisho became Empress in 1629. When he had full power on the death of Hidetada in 1633, Iemetsu replaced his *daimyo* advisors with childhood friends, who are credited with introducing the *sankin kotai* system in which *daimyo* were required to reside for a time in Edo. The expense of maintaining two residences and family hostages in Edo reduced the chances of *daimyo* to become powerful. In 1637 Iemetsu bloodily suppressed a revolt against his anti-Christian policy. Over the 1630s Iemetsu issued a series of edicts restricting Japanese contact with the outside world which included expulsion of Europeans (*sakoku* – national seclusion). The Dutch East India Company was restricted to one ship per year in a visit to the manmade island of Dejima in Nagasaki harbour. Punishment for violation of edicts was death.

Shogun Iemetsu died in 1651 at 47, to be succeeded by his eldest son, ten year-old Tokugawa Ietsuna under five regents. After Iemetsu's death a conspiracy was uncovered of a rebellion by *ronin* (masterless *samurai*) who had not followed their masters into death (*junshi*). In 1652 the rebellion was savagely suppressed and an orientation of government towards civilian rule prevented further *ronin* troubles. The old Yoshiwara entertainment (red light) district burned down (along with much of the Edo) in the Meireki fire of 1657. When Ietsuna came of age in 1663 he retained ex-regents as advisors but the act of abolishing *junshi* appears to have been his own. In 1679 Ietsuna became ill and his younger brother Tsunayoshi won the succession discussions.

Tokugawa Tsunayoshi had not been raised as a warrior because he was so precocious that he could be a danger to his elder brothers. He was invested as shogun in 1681 and quickly took control by confiscating a fief because of misgovernment. In 1682 Tsunayoshi ordered his censors and police to ban prostitution, waitresses in tea houses and expensive fabrics. Gold and silver coins, which were used mainly for Chinese luxury goods, needed to be devalued in

1695 due to a shortage of gold and silver. He became religious, promoting Neo-Confucianism which led to a campaign to provide protection of stray dogs. There were so many dogs in Edo that the smell led to a pejorative title - *Dog Shogun*. In 1706 Edo was hit by a typhoon and in the following year Mt. Fuji erupted. Tsunayoshi had homosexual interests that had led to plans to adopt one his boys as successor. The shogun's wife tried to dissuade him from such action, but when this was in vain, killed Tsunayoshi and then herself in 1709.

Tokugawa Ienobu was the nephew of Tsunayoshi and powerful *daimyo* of Tofu who also was the preferred successor of Tsunayoshi's late wife. Shogun Ienobu abolished many controversial laws and edicts of his predecessor and discontinued censorship. He also improved relations with the imperial court by changing the rule that younger sons enter the priesthood, and allowing younger daughters to marry. Many court ceremonies were revived with financial grants from the *bakufu*. Ienobu died in 1712, succeeded by his infant son Ietsugu. The Shogunate probably peaked under Tokugawa Ienobu.

The regent for Ietsugu was the Confucian scholar Arai Hakuseki who had been Ienobu's main advisor. His first problem was that of inflation which had arisen after the devaluations of 1706-1711. This was solved by introducing currency reform during which export of specie was banned in 1715 to encourage trade substitution. Cash crops expanded to include cotton, tea, tobacco and sugarcane. Only thirty Chinese ships and two Japanese ships per year were allowed into the trading island of Dejima in Nagasaki. The *bakufu* increased the gold and silver content of coinage but this commenced deflation. Takagawa Ietsugu died in 1716 at the age of seven and extinguished the direct paternal line of Ieyasu. As successor, Tokugawa Yoshimune was the son of Tokugawa Mitsusada, of the Kii *gosanke* (hereditary branch), and still a great grandson of Ieyasu.

Tokugawa Yoshimune had been trying to deal with the excessive inherited debt of his home Kii province, so was well equipped to undertake financial reforms aimed at making the shogunate financially solvent. These included the formation of merchant guilds to allow efficient control and taxation of trade. In 1730 the Dojima Rice Market in Osaka was recognised by the *bakufu* to monitor rice and collect taxes. This led to the development of the world's first commodity futures market that would later lead to a securities exchange. In 1736 Japan abandoned the policy of restricting the money supply to conquer deflation. In 1720 Yoshimune relaxed rules on foreign books which had been forbidden since 1640.

In 1745 Yoshimune followed the precedent of Ieyasu to abdicate with the title of *Ogosho* in favour of his son Ieshige. This was not a popular choice since Ieshige suffered a severe speech defect however Yoshimune followed the Confucian principle of primogeniture. Basically uninterested in government, Ieshige allowed his chamberlain, Ooka Tadamitsu to run the shogunate. As often happens when bureaucrats govern, the shogunate suffered corruption and lost control of the mercantile class. Natural disasters and famine did not help. Ieshige followed the example of his father and abdicated in 1760 in favour of his eldest son, Tokugawa Ieharu. Another three cadet branches (*gosankyo*) were added to the previous three (*gosanke*) from which future shoguns could be selected if the main line were to die out.

Ieharu was plagued with natural disasters of volcanic eruptions, drought, flood, disease and famine as well as the great fire of Edo. Tanuma Okitsugu, as Chief Counsellor, was decision maker but is generally considered to have been corrupt in favour of merchants. However Ieharu's government was manipulated into filling the Tokugawa coffers. Okitsugu provided the basis for the rise of the merchant class at the expense of the *samurai*. Copper made the Sumitomo family rich but the Mitsui family was the richest in Japan. Some *samurai* families became merchants such as the Iwasaki family who later founded the Mitsubishi company. Ieharu died in 1786 to be succeeded by his adopted son Tokugawa Ienari.

Ienari is known mostly for his harem which produced over 75 children in his long fifty year reign. Although the reign suffered from the great fire of Kyoto in 1788, earthquakes and volcanic eruptions, the natural disasters were only slightly less than in his father's reign. Ienari's regent, Matsudaira Sadanobu, was administrative decision maker who tried to fight corruption and excesses, by introducing Kansei reforms. He had some success in recovering the finances of the shogunate but was not politically popular and resigned in 1812. The Great Tenpo famine of the 1830's commenced peasant unrest which was to lead to rebellious breakouts. Ienari died in 1837 to be succeeded by his second son, Tokugawa Ieyoshi.

Tokugawa Ieyoshi inherited instability and famine as crops continued to decline in unfavourable weather. Peasant rebellions were relatively small in size but were the harbingers of the end of the Tokugawa Shogunate. Mizuno Tadakuni became Chief Counsellor in 1839 and endeavoured to overhaul finances and social reforms with the Tenpo Reform. New coinage was issued and commodity price controls were lifted. Restrictions to entertainment were introduced but were lifted in 1845 when Tadakuni was removed from government after Edo Castle burned down in 1844.

In the midst of Japanese political problems, in 1853 Commodore Matthew Perry of the United States Navy arrived in Uraga Harbour near Edo with four black-hulled steam-ships. He was told to travel to Nagasaki but refused to move and threatened to use force to remove Japanese ships surrounding his vessels. He presented a letter from US President Fillmore demanding a trade treaty between the USA and Japan. Perry then left for China. Tokugawa Ieyoshi died in 1853 to be succeeded by his third son Tokugawa Iesada who was probably too physically weak to be fit for shogun. Perry returned in 1854 with a larger fleet. Perry signed the Convention of Kanagawa in March 1854. Iesada chose Ii Naosuke to be Chief Counsellor (*Tairo*) who believed a trade treaty was in the best interests of Japan. The Treaty of Kanagawa – Harris Treaty of 1858 allowed the establishment of foreign concessions, extraterritoriality for foreigners, and minimal import taxes for foreign goods. The Hitotsubashi faction prevented presentation of the treaty to the emperor for approval so Ii ordered the treaty to be signed without approval so as not to upset the Americans. The *bakufu* of Iesada was blamed for the unequal clauses of the Harris Treaty and the treaties which followed with the Dutch, Russians, British, and French.

In response to the internal disputes of the shogunate, Emperor Komei began to assert himself to regain powers that his ancestors had relinquished to the shogunate. In 1858 a shogunate delegation under Hayashi Akira sought advice from the emperor about the Harris Treaty in a break with tradition. Komei opposed opening Japan to Western powers but realised in 1859 that there was no alternative to acceptance of the treaty. In 1863 Tokugawa Iemochi travelled to Kyoto in procession with 3000 retainers in response to the emperor's summons. He was the first *shogun* in 230years to visit the imperial capital. The reception and the emperor's visit to shrines with the shogun, demonstrated that a new order was developing.

Many feudal daimyos opposed the shogunate's open door policy to foreign trade in a *sonno joi* movement called *"Revere the Emperor, Expel the Barbarians"*. In March 1863 Emperor Komei issued an edict to expel the barbarians. The shogunate had no intention of enforcing the edict and was attacked. The traditional Tokugawa enemy Chosu clan opened fire on foreign ships traversing Shimonoseki Strait in June 1863. Naval forces of the USA and France retaliated, supported by the shogunate. Diplomatic overtures by the USA, France, Britain and Holland dragged on while *sonno joi* supporters destroyed foreign property. Following an attack by an international fleet in 1864 the Chosu forces surrendered. Inability of the *bakufu* to pay the huge claim for indemnity became pressure to have the emperor to ratify the treaties. Japan was in a precarious position when Tokugawa Iemochi died of beriberi in 1866 to be succeeded by Tokugawa Yoshinobu in January 1867. Only twenty days later Emperor Komei died to be succeeded by his fourteen year-old son Mutsuhito as Emperor Meiji.

In November 1867 Yoshinobu was persuaded to resign as *shogun* in favour of the Emperor. In line with the traditional Tokugawa Neo-Confucianist beliefs, he put the unity of Japan before his personal interests. There was to be a national governing council which Yoshinobu was to lead. Shogunate enemies obtained a court edict stripping Yoshinobu of all titles and land. Yoshinobu sent an army to deliver his letter of objections to the imperial court, but left the field when the Chosa and Satsuma forces flew the Imperial banner. In January 1868 Emperor Meiji announced the restoration of Imperial rule.

The Dutch Republic and Dutch East India Company 1602-1750

Long sea voyages of the sixteenth century suffered from loss of ships and crew, not the least from the disease of scurvy. Voyages were often undertaken by companies which offered shares to risk capitalists. Following a 1595 expedition to Java, numerous fleets financed by joint-stock companies obtained cargoes of Portuguese loot and spices from South East Asia that resulted in journey profits up to 200 percent. By 1601 fourteen Dutch fleets of sixty-five vessels and eight different companies were able to sail south. In 1602 an agreement was struck to create the United East India Company (*Vereenigde Oost-Indische Compagnie - VOC*) as a limited liability company which had the monopoly for twenty-one years of all lands east of the Cape of Good Hope and west of the straits of Magellan, including the rights to wage war and conclude peace.

The warehouses of Amsterdam distributed grains from the Baltic, furs from Russia, timber from Norway, sperm oil from the Arctic, sugar from Brazil, salt and wines from France, beaver skins from North America and spices from the East Indies. The mercantile oligarchy, under Pensionary Oldenbarneveldt, was powerful at that time, and negotiated the Treaty of Antwerp 1609. The States-General of the United Provinces were practically in control of the Dutch East

India Company (VOC) and the Dutch West India Company (WIC). Maurits of Nassau, then Prince of Orange, *stadtholder* and Lieutenant General/Admiral of the Union, decided to occupy towns and have their governments replaced by more amenable rulers. Oldenbarneveldt was executed.

VOC Governor-General Pieterszoon Coen in Asia decided to set up the company main post in Java closer to the travel routes than the first post in the Moluccas. His forces took Jayakarta from the natives in 1619, and on the ruins of the city, built Batavia, named after the Germanic ancestors of the Dutch. The trading post in America, New Amsterdam on the Hudson River, was well planned in advance by WIC directors and included the payment of sixty guilders for the land to the fiscally naïve native Manhattan Indians. The Netherland Antilles were established in the Caribbean for sugar plantations. The privateering nature of the WIC was revealed when it captured the Spanish silver fleet in 1628.

The VOC under Coen commenced an intra-Asiatic trade system in the 1620s to overcome a shortage of precious metals for Asian spices. The VOC used a large portion of its profits to build up trading capital to allow Asian trade. Through intrigue, the VOC replaced the Portuguese as the monopolists of Japan in 1639. Silver and copper from Japan were used to trade with India and China for silk, cotton, textiles and porcelain. These commodities were then either traded for spices or shipped back to Holland for trade in Europe.

Maurits died in 1625 during a siege, to be succeeded as *stadtholder* by his younger brother, Fredrik Henrik, who adopted all non-hereditary appointments. The naval victory over the Spanish fleet in the Battle of the Downs 1639 effectively ended Spanish maritime dominance. Unfortunately the Spanish eclipse also meant less money supply in the Netherlands from Spanish military expenditure. The Eighty Years War was finally ended by the Treaty of Munster in 1648 despite the objections of Wilhelm II of Orange, the son of Fredrik Henrik. In the same year, the Thirty Years War ended with the Peace of Westphalia which recognised the independence from Holy Empire of the Netherlands and Switzerland. Wilhelm wanted to resume war with Spain in accord with a French alliance. He secretly negotiated with France and worked for restoration in England of Charles II. He was obviously against the reduction of military forces under the Treaty of Munster because it would reduce his power. The province of Holland wanted to reduce military forces. In 1650 Wilhelm tried to enforce his will by imprisoning eight members of the Holland provincial assembly and ordering a force to take Amsterdam.

After the English Civil War it was natural that the anti-royalist regents running Holland did not want to appoint a *stadtholder* after Wilhelm II, so began the period called the First Stadtholderless Period under the Grand Pensionary (*raadpensionaris*) of Holland, Johan de Witt and the mayor/regent of Amsterdam, Cornelis De Graeff. Republican Protestant Holland was sure that their long alliance with non-royalist Protestant England against Catholic Spain would stand them in good stead. They failed to consider the resentment of English merchants over the dominance of the Dutch mercantile fleet. In 1651 the English Parliament voted in the Navigation Act which allowed imports to England only in English ships or those from the originating country. The Act was mainly aimed at the Dutch and was used to take Dutch ships by English privateers. War was declared by England in 1652 and it proved to be a naval war. The First Anglo-Dutch War was negotiated to an end in 1654.

In 1652 the VOC sent Jan van Riebeeck to establish a way-station in Table Bay, South Africa to support ships en route to the Dutch East Indies. *Fort de Goede Hoop* was established with a settlement that became *Kaapstad* (Cape Town). The Second Anglo Dutch War was really an extension of the First. Fighting had continued between Dutch and English trading empires. Privateers began attacking Dutch merchantmen. In late 1664 the English attacked the Dutch Smyrna fleet. Charles II declared war in 1665. The famous Admiral De Ruyter returned from America to command the Dutch fleet.

In the Far East, the Dutch East India Company (VOC) swept the English East India Company (EIC) from the seas of Indonesia. After a Dutch daring raid on London in 1667 the English had no option but to sue for peace. From 1670 the highly profitable trade with Japan started to decline when the shogunate limited the export of precious metals. The turmoil between the Ming and Manchu dynasties curtailed the Chinese silk trade. The inter-Asian trade was therefore in trouble even before the Third Anglo-Dutch War (1672-1674) affected trade with Europe.

By mid 1672 Wilhelm III had been appointed *stadtholder* and Captain-General of the Dutch army. De Witt resigned. The First Stadtholderless Period was over. In 1677 Charles II attempted to gain Protestant support in England by marrying brother James' daughter Mary Stuart to her cousin Wilhelm III of Orange-Nassau.

In the 1680s the VOC followed its competitor EIC by diversifying into lower margin commodities such as tea, coffee and sugar. Around the turn of the century the VOC had access to low cost capital that should have allowed it to surge ahead of its competitors, but the management was mired in the regent class which had lost touch with its merchant base. The VOC base in Batavia, Indonesia, should have been shifted closer to the sources of tea and coffee away from the spices which no longer attracted the monopolistic high profits.

English invasion prospects had been raised in both countries by 1688 when Wilhelm apparently assembled an expeditionary force for England. He had assessed that France was otherwise occupied so would not be an immediate problem to Holland. English public opinion became anti-Stuart over a trial of bishops opposing James religious policy. A group of political figures, known afterwards as the Immortal Seven, invited Wilhelm formally to invade England in the Glorious Revolution. In 1689 the English House of Commons made William accept a Bill of Rights and the Parliament passed the Declaration of Right offering William and Mary the right to rule as Joint Sovereigns.

Wilhelm's death in 1702 without issue produced problems in Holland then being run by Grand Pensionary Anthonie Hensius. The appointment of another *stadtholder*, especially Wilhelm's nephew Frederik of Prussia, might derail trade negotiations with France and Spain. It was decided to enter into the Second Stadtholderless Period where regents of the old States-Party were restored to their old positions. Dutch dominance probably peaked under Wilhelm III in 1702.

The end of the War of Spanish Succession under the Treaty of Utrecht in 1713 also marked the end of the Dutch Republic as a major European player. Anthonie Van de Heim became Grand Pensionary in 1736 and allowed the Republic to drift into the War of Austrian Succession. The War came to an untidy conclusion in 1747 but not before Wilhelm IV of Orange was appointed stadtholder and Captain General.

The economic decline became apparent from 1748 as did the fall in Dutch power in the face of the great powers of Prussia, Russia, France, England and Austria. In Asia the VOC had to ask for military assistance for the first time. The combined forces were not enough to save India, and Trincomalee in Sri Lanka (Ceylon). In 1810 The Netherlands were annexed into the French Empire.

England was not a dominant culture during the period 1600-1700 not the least because of Civil Wars and the competition from the Dutch republic.

Hohenzollem Dynasty of Prussia-Germany 1417-1918

In 1417 Friedrich Hohenzollern, Burgrave of Nuremberg, purchased Brandenburg, one of the seven Electorates of the Holy Roman Empire, from Emperor Sigismund. Under Elector John George (1571-1598) the lands of Brandenburg developed a Lutheran character. The Hohenzollern rulers sought lands through marriage. Elector Joachim II (1535-1571) married Princess Hedwig of Poland in 1535. The King of Poland was suzerain of the Duchy of Prussia, a Baltic principality that had been controlled by the Teutonic Order until its secularisation in 1525. Joachim succeeded in have his sons named as secondary heirs to Prussia. In 1603 Elector Joachim Friedrich persuaded the Polish king to grant him regency powers over Prussia. His son John Sigismund married Anna of Prussia in 1594. Joachim Friedrich married Anna, the younger sister of his son's wife, who had a claim to the inheritance of the Rhenish duchy Julich-Kleve.

The Hohenzollern rise to prominence commenced in 1640 when the Great Elector Friedrich Wilhelm commenced to rebuild Brandenburg-Prussia after the Thirty Years War. Twenty year-old Elector Friedrich Wilhelm inherited the devastated Margravate of Brandenburg, the Duchy of Cleves, the County of Mark, and the Duchy of Prussia. He had been educated in law, history and politics during long sojourns in the Dutch Republic. He returned to the ruined city of Berlin in 1643 and managed to rebuild his war-ravaged territories. In contrast to the religious disputes that disrupted the internal affairs of other European states, Brandenburg-Prussia benefited from the policy of religious tolerance adopted by Friedrich Wilhelm. With the help of French subsidies, he built up an army to defend the country based on the drill-book of Prince Maurice of Orange. After 1648 Brandenburg was the second-largest German territory after the Habsburg monarchy. However the Prussian state did not commence to dominate until the rule of King Friedrich *the Great* in 1740.

Although he was the Margrave and Prince-elector of Brandenburg and the Duke of Prussia, Friedrich III (1688-1713) desired the more prestigious title of king. However, according to Germanic law at that time, no kingdoms could exist within the Holy Roman Empire, with the exception of the Kingdom of Bohemia. Friedrich persuaded Leopold I, Archduke of Austria and Holy Roman Emperor, to allow Prussia to be elevated to a kingdom. This agreement was ostensibly given in exchange for an alliance against King Louis XIV of France in the War of the Spanish Succession. In 1701 Friedrich crowned himself King Friedrich I in Prussia in the city of Konigsberg. The House of Hohenzollern in Brandenburg-Prussia now enjoyed a pre-eminence among the Protestant dynasties of Germany.

Brandenburg and Prussia had maintained separate governments and seats of power in Berlin and Königsberg respectively until 1701, when Friedrich I consolidated them into one government. After ascending the throne Friedrich founded a new city southerly adjacent to Dorotheenstadt and named it after himself, the Friedrichstadt. Apart from initiating his royal court, was nothing much more was attained before his death in 1713. The urbane King Friedrich Wilhelm I drastically reduced the costly ceremonial royal court established by his father. Together with, or despite, a group of male counsellors, officials and military officers (known as the Tobacco Ministry) he continued to centralise and improve Prussia. He replaced mandatory military service among the middle class with an annual tax, and subordinated the nobility through military service. The officer corps was recruited from the provincial elites and trained through academies integrated into the central Cadet Corps School in Berlin. His rule was absolutist and he was a firm autocrat. He practiced rigid economy, never started a war, and at his death in 1740 there was a large surplus in the royal treasury.

King Friedrich II was raised since infancy by his authoritarian father to become a soldier. Unfortunately there was much "tough love" that resulted in beatings. After Friedrich had attempted to flee to England with his friend, Hans von Katte, he was forced to witness Katte's execution and imprisoned in Küstrin fortress for two months. Under Austrian influence Friedrich was granted a royal pardon and released from his cell in 1730. The crown prince returned to Berlin after finally being released from his tutelage at Küstrin in 1732. When Friedrich ascended the throne at twenty-eight as "King in Prussia" in 1740, his goal was to modernise and unite his vulnerably disconnected lands. He was married to Elisabeth of Brunswick-Bevern in name only.

Friedrich declined to endorse the Pragmatic Sanction of 1713, a legal mechanism to ensure the inheritance of the Habsburg domains by Maria Theresa of Austria. The War of Austrian Succession began in 1740, when Friedrich invaded and quickly occupied Silesia that was to have been Maria Theresa's inheritance. He had inherited an army of 80,000 men rigorously trained and well equipped, together with a substantial war-chest. At least one reason for Friedrich's sole decision was to pre-empt action by Saxony to link their state to Poland. Friedrich strongly suspected that the Austrians would start another war in an attempt to recover Silesia. Accordingly, he quickly made another alliance with the French and pre-emptively invaded Bohemia in 1744. Friedrich marched straight for Prague and laid siege to the city. Three days after the fall of Prague, Friedrich's troops were again on the march into the heart of central Bohemia. In 1745, Friedrich trapped a joint force of Saxons and Austrians that had crossed the mountains to invade Silesia and defeated them at the Battle of Hohenfriedberg. Once again, Friedrich's stunning victory on the battlefield caused his enemies to seek peace terms. Under the terms of the Treaty of Dresden, signed in 1745, Austria was forced to adhere to the terms of the Treaty of Breslau giving Silesia to Prussia.

The acquisition of Silesia permanently altered the political balance of the Holy Roman Empire and thrust Prussia into power politics, although Prussia was a non-combatant in the remainder of the War of Austrian Succession. Russia was alarmed at the Prussian success and in 1746 entered into an alliance with Vienna.

In 1756 following the collapse of the Anglo-Austrian Alliance, Friedrich swiftly made an alliance with Great Britain at the Convention of Westminster. As neighbouring countries began conspiring against him, Friedrich was determined to strike first. In August 1756 his well-prepared army crossed the frontier and pre-emptively invaded Saxony, thus beginning the Seven Years' War. The Seven Years War occurred, not the least because the Russo-Austrian Alliance became entangled with the conflict between the Austrian ally, Britain, and France. Facing a coalition which included Austria, France, Russia, Saxony, Sweden and several minor German states, and having only Great Britain, Hesse, Brunswick and Hanover as his allies, Friedrich narrowly kept Prussia in the war despite having his territories repeatedly invaded. The sudden death of Empress Elizabeth of Russia led to the succession of the pro-Prussian Peter III which in turn caused the collapse of the anti-Prussian coalition.

Friedrich frequently led his military forces personally and had six horses shot from under him during battle. Friedrich is often admired as one of the greatest tactical military geniuses of all time, especially for his usage of the oblique order of battle. Napoleon was a later fan. Even more important were his operational successes, especially preventing the unification of numerically superior opposing armies and being at the right place at the right time to keep enemy armies out of Prussian core territory. The brave actions in war of the Junker nobility officers earned them a special place within Friedrich's state. The returned non-commissioned men were rewarded with low-wage jobs with the excise, customs and the tobacco monopoly, together with minor government posts.

Empress Catherine II took the Imperial Russian throne in 1762 after the murder of her husband, Peter III. Catherine was staunchly opposed to Prussia, while Friedrich disapproved of Russia, whose troops had been allowed to freely cross the Polish-Lithuanian Commonwealth during the Seven Years' War. Despite the two monarchs' dislike of each other, Friedrich and Catherine signed a defensive alliance in 1764 which guaranteed Prussian control of Silesia in return for Prussian support for Russia against Austria or the Ottoman Empire. In the First Partition of Poland in 1772, Friedrich claimed most of the Polish province of Royal Prussia (West Prussia). However, the newly created province of West Prussia connected East Prussia and Farther Pomerania and granted Prussia control of the mouth of the Vistula River. Friedrich began titling himself "King of Prussia".

Friedrich quickly began improving the infrastructure of West Prussia, reforming its administrative and legal code, and improving the school system. 750 new schools were built from 1772–1775. Both Protestant and Roman Catholic teachers taught in West Prussia, and teachers and administrators were encouraged to be able to speak both German and Polish.

During his reign, Friedrich helped transform Prussia from a European backwater to an economically strong and politically reformed state. His conquest of Silesia helped to provide Prussia's fledgling industries with raw materials, and he protected these industries with high tariffs and minimal restrictions on domestic trade. Moreover, the developing technology of the time enabled him to create new farmland through a massive drainage program in the country's Oderbruch marsh-land. With the help of French experts, he organised a system of indirect taxation, which provided the state with more revenue than direct taxation. One of Friedrich's greatest achievements included the control of grain prices, whereby government storehouses would enable the civilian population to survive in needy regions, where the harvest was poor.

In 1785, Friedrich II signed a Treaty of amity and commerce with the United States of America, recognising the independence of the United States. The agreement included a novel clause, whereby the two leaders of the executive branches of either country guaranteed a special and humane detention for prisoners of war. Friedrich *the Great* died in the palace of Sanssouci in 1786. He left a Prussia with the third largest army in Europe supported patriotically by a population of only 5.8million.

Friedrich *the Great's* nephew and successor, the much married Friedrich Wilhelm II, was the antithesis of his uncle. His accession to the throne was followed by a series of measures for lightening the burdens of the people, reforming the oppressive French system of tax-collecting introduced by Friedrich and encouraging trade by the diminution of customs dues and the making of roads and canals. This gave the new king much popularity with the masses. Friedrich Wilhelm also terminated his predecessor's state monopolies for coffee and tobacco and the sugar monopoly.

A formal alliance with Austria was signed in 1792. Friedrich Wilhelm was hampered, however, by want of funds, and his counsels were distracted by the affairs of Poland, which promised a richer booty than was likely to be gained by an anti-revolutionary crusade into France. The insurrection in Poland that followed the partition of 1793, and the threat of the isolated intervention of Russia, hurried Friedrich Wilhelm into the separate Treaty of Basel with the French Republic (1795), which was regarded by the great monarchies as a betrayal, and left Prussia morally isolated in Europe on the eve of the struggle between the monarchical principle and the new republican creed of the French Revolution. Although the area ruled by the Prussian state reached a new peak under his rule after the third partition of Poland in 1795, these territories included parts of Poland such as Warsaw with virtually no German population whatsoever, bringing with it problems of integration. Prussia was financially exhausted. The internationally distrusted Friedrich Wilhelm II died in 1797, succeeded by his son Friedrich Wilhelm III.

The new King showed that he was earnest in his good intentions by cutting down the expenses of the royal establishment, dismissing his father's ministers, and reforming the most oppressive abuses of the late reign. Disgusted with the moral debauchery of his father's court (in both political intrigues and sexual affairs), Friedrich Wilhelm's first endeavour was to restore morality to his dynasty. He was a hesitant and cautious individual who hated war, and was out of his depth in the international crises.

The geopolitical revolution stimulated by the French in 1797 broke up the Holy Roman Empire, the formal end of which occurred in 1806. At first Friedrich Wilhelm and his advisors attempted to pursue a policy of neutrality in the Napoleonic Wars. Prussia succeeded in keeping out of the Third Coalition in 1805, although with much ministerial debate. The quality of the Prussian army had declined due to its dependence on foreign troops. Eventually Friedrich Wilhelm was swayed by the belligerent attitude of his beautiful Queen Luise, who led Prussia's pro-war party, and entered into war in 1806. At the Battle of Jena-Auerstädt, the French defeated the Prussian army led by Friedrich Wilhelm, and the Prussian army collapsed. Berlin was occupied. The royal family fled to Memel, East Prussia, where they fell on the mercy of Emperor Alexander I of Russia.

In 1811 Chancellor Hardenberg convened an Assembly of Notables to find a way of radical fiscal reform to deal with French imposed debt. The Assembly failed, as did several other semi-democratic assemblies in 1812 and 1814. Hardenberg had to apply his own solutions to state debt. The Prussians reregulated commerce, manufacture, internal trade and labour. In 1813, following Napoleon's disastrous Russian invasion, Friedrich Wilhelm turned against France and signed an alliance with Russia at Kalisz, although he had to flee Berlin, still under French occupation. Prussian troops (including conscripted *Landwehr*) played a key part in the victories of the allies in 1813 and 1814, and the King himself travelled with the main army of Prince Schwarzenberg, along with Emperors Alexander of Russia and Francis of Austria. Although the army had relatively poor uniforms and equipment, the reformed command system worked well under Generals Blucher, Yorck, Kleist and Bulow. The military award of the Iron Cross for valour was initiated.

At the Congress of Vienna, Friedrich Wilhelm's ministers succeeded in securing important territorial increases for Prussia, although they failed to obtain the annexation of all of Saxony, as they had wished. The German Confederal Treaty of 1815 (revised 1820) was largely an Austrian conception forming the German Confederation of thirty-eight states (later thirty-nine) under a Federal Diet in Frankfurt. The Confederation did not provide Berlin with dominant powers but was open-ended enough to allow limited hegemony. A German Customs Union came into effect in 1834.

Following the war, Friedrich Wilhelm turned towards political reaction, abandoning the promises he had made in 1813 to provide Prussia with a constitution, although provincial diets were allowed. He now had a Cabinet of ministers who were trying to create a military alliance with the southern German states which would undermine Austrian influence. Austrian diplomacy could not be overcome and the King had a coterie of personal advisers not in favour. Friedrich Wilhelm III's daughter Charlotte was married to Grand Duke Nicholas who became Tsar Nicholas I in 1825. During the 1830s the provincial diets provided a venue for dissidents seeking a national diet. Friedrich Wilhelm III died in 1840 in Berlin.

The new king, Friedrich Wilhelm IV, initially moved to repress dissent with the army, but, after deaths of demonstrators, decided to recall the troops and place himself at the head of the movement. In 1848 he committed himself to German unification, formed a liberal government, convened a National Assembly, and ordered that a constitution be drawn up. When the political situation stabilised he dissolved the Assembly. It was his Romantic aspiration to re-establish the medieval German Reich comprising smaller, semi-sovereign monarchies under the limited authority of a Habsburg emperor. Therefore Friedrich Wilhelm would only accept the imperial crown after being elected by German princes to do so, as per the old empire's ancient customs. Throughout Brandenburg demonstrations were curbed by the army.

He created a parliament with two chambers, an aristocratic upper house and an elected lower house. The lower house was elected by all taxpayers, but in a three-tiered system based on the amount of taxes paid so that true universal suffrage was denied. The constitution also reserved for the king the power of appointing all ministers, re-established the conservative district assemblies and provincial diets, and guaranteed that the bureaucracy and the military remained firmly in the hands of the king. This constitution, adopted in 1850, remained in effect until the dissolution of the Prussian kingdom in 1918. The Prussian Assembly became the State Diet (*Landtag*).

In 1849 the Frankfurt Assembly of the German Confederation voted to approve a monarchical constitution for the new Germany and for Friedrich Wilhelm IV as German Emperor. The King declined the honour. After military problems instigated by the Elector of Hesse-Kassel caused confrontation with Prussian troops, the old German Confederation was restored in 1851. Prussia was the only major European power to remain neutral in the Crimean War (1854-56).

A stroke in 1857 left the king partially paralysed and largely mentally incapacitated, and his brother Wilhelm served as regent from 1858 until the king's death in 1861, at which point he acceded the throne himself as Wilhelm I. He had worn military uniform since age six and as a young Captain he had fought in the Napoleonic war. The fight against France left a lifelong impression on him, in particular causing a long-standing antipathy against the French. As Prince Regent, Wilhelm, swore an oath of office on the Prussian constitution and promised to preserve it "solid and inviolable". His appointment of the liberal Prince Adolf zu Hohenlohe-Ingelfingenas as Minister President initiated the "New Era" in Prussia

Wilhelm inherited the conflict between Friedrich Wilhelm and the liberal *Landtag*. He was considered a politically neutral person as he intervened less in politics than his brother. In 1861 the *Landtag* refused an increase in the military budget that was required to pay for the already implemented reform of the army.

Wilhelm dissolved parliament and called for new elections. When his request for reform, backed by his Minister of War Albrecht von Roon was refused in 1862, Wilhelm first considered resigning but his son, the Crown Prince, advised strongly against it. Then, on the advice of Roon, Wilhelm appointed Otto von Bismarck to the office of Minister President in order to force through the proposals.

Otto Eduard Leopold, Prince of Bismarck, Duke of Lauenburg was known as Otto Von Bismarck. He had been chosen as a representative of the Prussian legislature in 1847, age 32, and openly advocated the monarch's divine right to rule. In 1851, Friedrich Wilhelm IV appointed Bismarck as Prussia's envoy to the Diet of the German Confederation in Frankfurt. Bismarck gave up his elected seat in the *Landtag*, but was appointed to the Prussian House of Lords a few years later. He grew to be more accepting of the notion of a united German nation. Bismarck also worked to maintain the friendship of Russia and a working relationship with Napoleon III's France to threaten Austria and prevent France from allying with Russia. As Prussia's ambassador to the Russian Empire, he watched impotently as France drove Austria out of Lombardy during the Italian War of 1859.

The Franco-Prussian War (1870) was a great success for Prussia. The German army, under nominal command of the King but controlled by Chief of Staff Moltke, won victory after victory. The Prussian needle-gun was no longer an advantage because the French used a similar rifle, as well as an early machine gun. The Prussians had introduced rifled cannon incorporating the latest technology so they had superior artillery.

King Wilhelm of Prussia was proclaimed German Emperor (*Kaiser Wilhelm I*) in 1871 in the Hall of Mirrors in the Château de Versailles. The new German Empire was a federation but each of its 25 constituent states (kingdoms, grand duchies, duchies, principalities, and free cities) retained some autonomy. The King of Prussia, as German Emperor, was not sovereign over the entirety of Germany; he was only *primus inter pares*, or first among equals. But he held the presidency of the *Bundesrat*, which met to discuss policy presented from the Chancellor (whom the president appointed). Wilhelm viewed his Kingship of Prussia as much more important than the title of German Emperor. Despite possessing considerable power as *Kaiser*, Wilhelm left the task of governing empire mostly to his Chancellor and limited himself to representation, embodying the dignity of the state and approving Bismarck's policies.

The popular Wilhelm died on in 1888 in Berlin after a short illness. Many people considered the royal family the personification of "the old Prussia" and liked their austere and simple lifestyle. Wilhelm I left the throne to his son, Friedrich III. The new monarch was already suffering from an incurable throat cancer and died after reigning for only 99 days. Under the leadership of Wilhelm I and his Minister President Otto von Bismarck, Prussia achieved the unification of Germany and the establishment of the German Empire. I have placed the peak of the Prussian dominance at 1888 on the death of Kaiser Wilhelm I.

The new Emperor, Friedrich's son Wilhelm II, opposed Bismarck's careful foreign policy, preferring vigorous and rapid expansion to enlarge Germany's "place in the sun". Wilhelm also opposed Bismarck's policy to make the anti-Socialist laws permanent. After a blazing row with Wilhelm, Bismarck wrote a blistering letter of resignation (published only after Bismarck's death), decrying Wilhelm's interference in foreign and domestic policy. Bismarck resigned at Wilhelm II's insistence in 1890, at the age of 75, to be succeeded as Chancellor of Germany and Minister-President of Prussia by Leo von Caprivi, who in turn was replaced by Chlodwig, Prince of Hohenlohe-Schillingsfürst, in 1894.

As part of Kaiser Wilhelm's "new course" in foreign policy, Caprivi abandoned Bismarck's military, economic, and ideological cooperation with Russia, but was unable to forge a close relationship with Britain. He successfully promoted the reorganisation of the German military. The rejection in the Diet by the Conservatives intensified, accompanied with constant public attacks by retired Bismarck. Caprivi also lost the support of the National Liberals and Progressives in a legislative defeat of 1892 on an educational bill providing denominational board schools, a failed attempt to re-integrate the Catholic Centre Party. After the *Kulturkampf* Caprivi had to resign as Prussian Minister President which in turn led to his dismissal also as Chancellor in 1894. Chodwig, Prince of Hohenlohe, replaced Caprivi, in spite of his advanced years. In general, during his term of office, the personality of the Chancellor was less conspicuous in public affairs than in the case of either of his predecessors.

In appointing Caprivi and then Hohenlohe, Wilhelm hoped to exert decisive influence in the government of the empire implementing "personal rule". In 1897 Wilhelm, who was looking for a new Secretary of State for Foreign Affairs, met Bernhard Heinrich Karl Martin von Bülow who met his expectations. Wilhelm began to concentrate upon his real agenda; the creation of a German navy that would rival that of Britain and enable Germany to declare itself a world power. A German navy would politically offset the dominance of the Prussian military. Wilhelm II embarked on major travels across Empire speaking at gatherings far more than any Prussian had previously exposed himself. He became a *media monarch*. Over time the practical effect was a gradual erosion of political pronouncement from the throne.

The Prussian military remained a praetorian guard under the personal command of the king. There was no imperial minister of war, simply a Prussian minister of war, appointed by the king, and required to swear an oath of loyalty to Prussia, not empire. The military cabinet reported directly to the monarch. There was perpetual uncertainty between the parameters of civil and military authority particularly in the new colonies. In practice military authority was superior, supported by Wilhelm.

Theobald Theodor Friedrich Alfred von Bethmann Hollweg became Chancellor in 1909 and pursued a policy of détente with Britain, hoping to come to some agreement that would put a halt to the two countries' ruinous naval arms race. He failed, largely due to the opposition of German Naval Minister Alfred von Tirpitz. Despite the increase in tensions due to the Second Moroccan Crisis of 1911, Bethmann Hollweg did improve relations with Britain to some extent, working with British foreign secretary Sir Edward Grey to alleviate tensions during the Balkan Crises of 1912-1913, and negotiating treaties over an eventual partition of the Portuguese colonies and the Berlin-Baghdad railway. Wilhelm began to spread alarm in the chancelleries of Europe with his increasingly eccentric views on foreign affairs.

Following the assassination of Archduke Franz Ferdinand in Sarajevo in 1914, Bethmann Hollweg and Foreign Secretary Gottlieb von Jagow were instrumental in assuring Austria of Germany's unconditional support regardless of Austria's actions against Serbia. Wilhelm offered to support Austria-Hungary in crushing the *Black Hand*, the secret organisation that had plotted the killing. Austro-Hungarian ministers and generals had already convinced the 84-year-old Emperor Franz Joseph I of Austria to sign a declaration of war against Serbia. As a direct consequence, Russia began a general mobilisation to attack Austria in defence of Serbia. When it became clear that Germany would experience a war on two fronts and that the United Kingdom would enter the war if Germany attacked France through neutral Belgium, the panic-stricken Wilhelm attempted to redirect the main attack against Russia.

In the original 1905 Schlieffen plan, Germany would attack the (supposed) weaker enemy first, meaning France. The plan supposed that it would take a long time before Russia was ready for war. Defeating France had been easy for

Prussia in the Franco-Prussian War in 1870. At the 1914 border between France and Germany, an attack at this more southern part of France could be stopped by the French fortresses along the border. British involvement was inevitable. Bethmann Hollweg appeared to have some second thoughts, and he took half-hearted measures to prevent an all out war, until Russia's mobilisation took the matter out of his hands. During the war, Bethmann Hollweg has usually been seen as having generally attempted to pursue a relatively moderate policy, but having been frequently outflanked by the military leaders, who played an increasingly important role in the direction of all German policy. The successful Battle of Tannenberg against Russia was named after the first pre-Prussian battle in 1410 by Teutonic Knights, so as to promote German nationalism.

The military high command continued with its strategy even when it was clear that the Schlieffen plan had failed when western momentum was stopped by the First Battle of the Marne 1914. The Russians mobilised in 1914. Germany's war would be on two fronts. 1916 was characterised by two great battles on the Western front, at Verdun and Somme. The Germans became bogged down by Verdun.

By 1916 the Empire had effectively become a military dictatorship under the control of Field Marshal Paul von Hindenburg and General Erich Ludendorff. Over Bethmann Hollweg's objections, Hindenburg and Ludendorff forced the adoption of unrestricted submarine warfare in 1917, which led to the United States' entry into the war. In 1917, Hindenburg and Ludendorff decided that Bethman-Hollweg was no longer acceptable to them as Chancellor and called upon the Kaiser to appoint somebody else. When asked whom they would accept, Ludendorff recommended Georg Michaelis. The Kaiser did not know Michaelis, but accepted the suggestion.

Michaelis became Chancellor of Germany as well as Minister President of Prussia--the only non-titled person to serve as chief minister of Prussia or Germany prior to the fall of the Hohenzollern monarchy. He remained in this position until late 1917, when he was forced to resign after coming under fire for refusing to commit himself by endorsing a resolution passed by the Reichstag favouring peace without annexation or indemnities. Wilhelm I chose to bow to the threats of resignation by von Hindenburg and Ludendorff rather than defend his Chancellor.

Wilhelm was at the Imperial Army headquarters in Spa, Belgium, when the uprisings in Berlin and other centres took him by surprise in late 1918. Mutiny among the ranks of his beloved *Kaiserliche Marine*, the imperial navy, profoundly shocked him. After the outbreak of the German Revolution, Wilhelm could not make up his mind whether or not to abdicate. Up to that point, he accepted that he would likely have to give up the imperial crown, but still hoped to retain the Prussian kingship. The unreality of this belief was revealed when, in the hope of preserving the monarchy in the face of growing revolutionary unrest, Chancellor Prince Maximilian von Baden announced Wilhelm's abdication of both titles on 9 November 1918. Prince Max himself was forced to resign later the same day.

Wilhelm,—now Wilhelm Hohenzollern, private citizen—, crossed the border and went into exile in the Netherlands, which had remained neutral throughout the war. Upon the conclusion of the Treaty of Versailles in early 1919, Article 227 expressly provided for the prosecution of Wilhelm "*for a supreme offence against international morality and the sanctity of treaties*", but Queen Wilhelmina refused to extradite him, despite appeals from the Allies.

In 1918 a coalition Prussian government was formed of the Social Democratic Party (SPD) and the left-wing socialist Independent SPD (USPD). Prussia no longer had the power to directly influence the other states. There was now a German executive of the national Republic, entirely separate from the new Free State of Prussia. In 1919, a national assembly was convened in Weimar, where a new constitution for the German Reich was written. In its fourteen years, the Weimar Republic faced numerous problems,

The collapse of Prussian-German dominant culture can be taken as the end of World War I in 1918 when Kaiser Wilhelm II abdicated, but definitely when the Weimar Republic was formed in 1919.

Although influential, the Austrian Empire/Austro-Hungary Empire was not dominant in the period under review.

I have assessed Nazi Germany and the Third Reich as a totalitarian state which had little connection to the Hohenzollern culture. It is my belief that Adolf Hitler and the National Socialist German Workers Party exploited the feelings of the German people 1933-1945 following the harsh terms imposed by the allies in the Treaty of Versailles. The Nazi period of dominance was insufficient to consider it as a dominant culture according to my guidelines.

Pattern of Rulers

The above mentioned dominant cultures were basically ruled by monarchs possibly influenced by bureaucracies that had some nascent democratic features.

The succeeding British Empire culture became ruled by a constitutional monarchy guided by a democratic parliament. The United States culture is ruled by a president guided by a democratic Congress. I believe that this form of leadership does not depart from the long cycle of dominance established under sole rulers, but will examine the patterns when assessing the future.

Leaders were diverse in their actions and cultures, but I have identified a common strength in the establishment of able bureaucracies which allowed the pattern of relatively just administration of their societies. Peaceful administration in turn provided the basis for prosperity when the country was not at war. Each culture went into decline when the leaders no longer strong enough to control their bureaucracies. Without strong rulers the bureaucrats often turned corrupt. Ineffective government also led to debt which compounded problems of dominance. The decline of the cultures tended to stem mainly from internal pressure, which sometimes allowed the fatal fall from external intrusion. Peasant revolts were a common factor prior to collapse, but the organised bureaucracies of government had tended to become fossilised and unable to deal with complex problems such as economic breakdowns. Major wars that provided the final blow tended to shorten the time of decline from the peak of dominance.

Cohesive Religion

The Tsardom of Russia had the cohesive religion of the Russian Orthodox Church.

The dominant religious beliefs during the Ming dynasty were the various forms of Chinese folk religion and the Three Teachings – Confucianism, Taoism, and Buddhism. Islam had won a number of converts among the Mongols in China, but in the sixteenth century the Chinese Mongol tribes were mainly Lamaist Buddhist. Confucianist Emperor Hongwu, whose wife was descended from a Muslim family, was tolerant of Islam. The advent of the Ming was initially devastating to Christianity. In his first year, the Hongwu Emperor declared the eighty-year-old Franciscan missions among the Yuan, heterodox and illegal. The later Ming saw a new wave of Christian – particularly Jesuit – missionaries arrive, who employed new western science and technology in their arguments for conversion.

All of Christian Europe had been Catholic until the German monk Martin Luther criticised the Catholic Church in 1517. Protestantism expanded rapidly in Germany where Holy Roman Emperor Karl V had only nominal power as emperor. By 1530 the Holy Empire was regarded by the Protestants as a tool of the Vatican and Jesuits. Protestants by then included the princes of Saxony, Hesse, Brandenburg, and Schleswig. The Catholic Habsburgs could no longer control Europe when Protestantism spread. The Spanish were unquestionably cohesively Catholic even before the reigns of Isabella and Ferdinand, but there were a minority of Jews and Muslims in the kingdoms. Isabel decreed forced conversion of Muslims and expulsion of Jews. In 1609 the Muslim converts were expelled from Spain. The expulsion depleted Spain of many skills. Religious intolerance coincided with decline of dominance.

The fifteenth century interpretation of the Koran saw the will of God impose the duty on Muslims to propagate Islam by force of arms. The Ottomans obeyed their religious duty with the same fervour that was to be seen by Catholics in Spain, but with more tolerance after victory. The form of religious toleration of the Ottoman Sunni Muslims was one of the strengths of empire. Islam was not forced upon the multi-cultural population, but non-Muslims (*dhimmi*) had to pay a tax to practice their religion. During the first decade of the sixteenth century, Shah Isma'il Safawi, ruler of Persia, broke the tradition of religious toleration when he imposed Shiism on his majority of Sunni subjects by force. The Shiite victors spread their religious war to Anatolia as part of a political war of supremacy. In 1514, Selim I *the Grim* ordered the massacre of 40,000 Anatolian Shi'ites, whom he considered heretics.

From the Safavid period onwards, the majority of Persians adopted Shi'a Islam, not the least because Shah Ismail I aimed at the destruction of Sunnism. Shah Isma'il's Shi'ism required the faithful to curse the memory of the first three caliphs who preceded Ali, which was offensive to Sunni Muslims. The forceful imposition of Shi'a Islam meant that Persia under the Abbasids had a cohesive, although intolerant, religion.

France was Catholic until the Protestant faith filtered from the east in the early 1500's. Lutherism circulated around Paris before official attention was paid, bur Calvinism became popular with the Huguenots. Any tolerance was shattered by the Catholic League sponsored by Felipe II of Spain through the de Guise family. Six Religious wars were fought before Catholicism again dominated as decreed by Louis XIV. Once again, religious expulsion of Protestants resulted in the loss to the country of many skills.

Hinduism had been the predominant religion of India since pre-history, with later lesser faiths of Jainism and Buddhism. When Islam invaded, Buddhism declined rapidly and many Hindus converted to Islam. In 1579 Sunni Muslim Shah Akbar declared that he was *Khalifa* and could issue decrees. He declared a prohibition on Shia-Sunni conflict. From the 1570s he began to move towards religious tolerance and against the Afghan *ulama* (religious body). He abolished taxes on Hindus and permitted repair and building of Hindu temples. In 1582 he sought to initiate a new religious movement, or ethical system – *Din-i-Ilahi* but had little support. Persian immigration to the Deccan spread the Shi'a Islam faith of the Safavid dynasty. Aurangzeb abandoned the liberal religious policies introduced by Akbar. Aurangzeb tried to create a Muslim state by rewarding conversion to Islam. He tried to reduce the number of Hindu officials. He pulled down more Hindu temples and reinstated the Hindu pilgrim tax.

In the Union of Utrecht of 1579, Holland and Zeeland were granted the right to accept only one religion (in practice, Calvinism). Every other province had the freedom to regulate the religious question as it wished, although the Union stated every person should be free in the choice of personal religion and that no person should be prosecuted based on religious choice. In practice, Catholic services in all provinces were quickly forbidden, and the Reformed Church became the "public" or "privileged" church in the Dutch Republic.

The Japanese Tokugawa government was guided by Confucian principles but the majority of the population was Buddhist. During the Tokugawa period, Confucianism emerged from Buddhist religious control. Buddhism, combined with neo-Confucianism, provided standards of social behaviour. Although not as powerful politically as it had been in the past, Buddhism was espoused by the upper classes. Proscriptions against Christianity benefited Buddhism in 1640 when the *bakufu* ordered everyone to register at a temple. The rigid separation of Tokugawa society into *han*, villages, wards, and households helped reaffirm local Shinto attachments. Shinto provided spiritual support to the political order and was an important tie between the individual and the community. Shinto also helped preserve a sense of national identity. Shinto eventually assumed an intellectual form as shaped by neo-Confucian rationalism and materialism. The *kokugaku* movement emerged from the interactions of these two belief systems. *Kokugaku* contributed to the emperor-centered nationalism of modern Japan and the revival of Shinto as a national creed in the eighteenth and nineteenth centuries.

Prussia was basically protestant Christian, Lutheran/Calvinist, for its long existence. Unfortunately there was underlying social tension initiated by Christian corporate oligarchies of Prussian towns in the eighteenth century. In 1837 major conflict occurred in the heavily Catholic Rhineland and in the eastern provinces with a large Catholic population of Poles. Bismarck launched an anti-Catholic *Kulturkampf* ("culture struggle") in Prussia in 1871.

By the time of Capitalist Regimes, religions had basically been well established but sects of established religions diversified and sometimes led to war. The best dominant cultures observed a basic cohesive religious preference but were tolerant of other religions and sects. Cultures were severely disrupted when wars were fought over religion but the disruption did not necessarily lead to the end of their regimes.

The Rule of Law

In the 1550s, Ivan IV of Muscovy declared a new law code (*Sudebnik*), which revised laws instituted by his grandfather Ivan *the Great*. The *Sudebnik* of 1550 liquidated judicial privileges of the aristocracy and strengthened the role of the system of the judicial bodies of the state. The *Sudebnik* provided the active participation of the elective representatives of local communities (rural heads, jurymen, *tselovalniki, dvorskie* etc.) in the legal proceedings.

Although the codification of Chinese law was largely completed by the *T'ang Code* of 624AD, throughout the centuries the Confucian foundations of the *T'ang Code* were retained, and indeed with some aspects of it strengthened by the later dynasties. There was no civil code separate from the criminal code, which led to the now discredited belief that traditional Chinese law had no civil law. The legal code, drawn up in the time of Hongwu, was known as the *"Code of the Great Ming"*. It was considered comprehensive and intelligible with emphasis on family relations. The law protected both slaves and free citizens.

In 1532 Holy Emperor Karl V issued his *Constitutio Criminalis Carolina*, a criminal code that attempted to safeguard the innocent from inquisitorial methods. However, the *Carolina* limited actual trials to a public ceremony at the end of the state's secretive inquisition. Trials were separate from the execution of punishment, but the actual deliberations were a secret matter controlled by the authorities. Punishment and execution were turned into public spectacle that validated the non-public courts. Public executions served to demonstrate that the people consented to a sentence that they could not control.

The Ottoman Empire was always organised around a system of local jurisprudence. Legal administration in the Ottoman Empire was part of a larger scheme of balancing central and local authority. The jurisdictional complexity of the Ottoman Empire was aimed to permit the integration of culturally and religiously different groups. The Ottoman system had three court systems: one for Muslims, one for non-Muslims, involving appointed Jews and Christians ruling over their respective religious communities, and the "trade court". The entire system was regulated from above by means of the administrative *Kanun*. The Islamic *Sharia* law system had been developed from a combination of the Qur'an; the Hadīth, or words of the prophet Muhammad; *ijmā'*, or consensus of the members of the Muslim community; *qiyas*, a system of analogical reasoning from earlier precedents; and local customs. Both systems were taught at the Empire's law schools, which were in Istanbul and Bursa. Mehmed II is recognised as the first Sultan to codify criminal and constitutional law. Suleiman *the Lawgiver* issued a single legal code covering the *Kanuns* (canonical legislation within Sharia' law) in criminal law, land tenure and taxation. The legal code was to last three hundred years.

In Safavid Persia there was little distinction between theology and jurisprudence, or between divine justice and human justice, and it all went under Islamic jurisprudence (*fiqh*). The legal system was built up of two branches: civil law, which had its roots in *sharia*, (received wisdom), and *urf*, meaning traditional experience, and very similar to the Western form of common law. While the *imams* and judges of law applied civil law in their practice, *urf* was primarily exercised by the local commissioners, who inspected the villages on behalf of the Shah, and by the Minister of Justice (*Divanbegi*). Criminal justice was entirely separate from civil law and was judged upon common law administered through the Minister of Justice, local governors and the Court minister (the *Nazir*).

French law developed from Roman-Canon law which in turn developed into the Napoleonic Code.

Akbar's Muslim Mughal rule was made acceptable to Hindus by the administration of different laws - *Sharia* law for Muslims and *Dharmashastra* law for Hindus. This was similar to the rule of the Visigoths in Spain centuries before, that allowed integration of the Goths and Roman Hispanics. The model of government in which the territories were under control of the Emperor, but largely independent under imperial vassals, would be followed by the English when they tried colonial government three hundred years later.

All the provinces of the Dutch Republic were autonomous and had their own government, the "States of the Province" which had their own laws.

The individual had no legal rights in Tokugawa Japan. The family was the smallest legal entity, and the maintenance of family status and privileges was of great importance at all levels of society. For example, the Edo period penal laws prescribed "non-free labour" or slavery for the immediate family of executed criminals in Article 17 of the *Gotōke reijō* (Tokugawa House Laws), but the practice never became common.

Laws and edicts issued by successive Prussian sovereigns after 1648 gradually subjected the patrimonial courts of the *Junker* lordships to territorial law in control of their peasants. In 1717 Friedrich Wilhelm I ordered that every court operate under the new Criminal Code (*Criminal-Ordnung*). The General Law Code (*Allgemeines Preußisches Landrecht*) was published in 1794 which provided structure of every conceivable transaction between one Prussian and another. This defined the laws affecting the noble Estate with privileged access to the highest courts of the land. The law characterised peasant subjects as "free persons of the state" but reinforced the existing structure of corporate and noble domination.

The common thread linking dominant cultures of the early Capitalist Era was a respect by the leaders for the rule of regulation or law promulgated to their citizens. The laws, and their enforcement, were not always fair and just, because, as in modern civilisation, leaders tended to interpret laws to favour political will. On balance however, the leaders' desire for a well regulated society meant that laws were made with an eye to acceptable precedent and enforced to produce an orderly society. All dominant societies from 1400 operated under rule of law which was an important factor in allowing the rule of monarchs over diversified populations.

Economics

Habsburgs

The Spanish economy flourished during the fifteenth century. Its increasing stability supported the new political trends and was in turn reinforced by them.

The result was the creation of the strongest nation-state in the Western world. The Catholic monarchs guided the economy by encouraging shipbuilding and protected local industry against foreign competition. Europe's money supply had greatly expanded from the 1460s when new silver mines in the Tyrol, Saxony and Bohemia produced great amounts of silver. In the 1480s civil war, Antwerp replaced Bruges as the marketplace for north-west Europe.

The first bullion from Peru arrived in 1533 but the Spanish government's share was still only 20%, compared to 10% from that of New Spain which had commenced in 1506. In Spain, where the impact of American treasure was comparatively large, the pace of inflation actually lagged behind other parts of Europe.

In 1543 Holy Emperor Karl V approved usury, lending at interest, in the Holy Roman Empire. From the 1540s, wars in the Netherlands were financed from bonds issued by various towns and provinces pledged against public revenue. The Spanish government kept going by mortgaging its annual treasure fleet before the ships arrived, to foreign bankers at ruinous rates of interest. By 1543 a large part of Castilian revenue simply went to pay the interest on a public debt that was soaring out of control. The reasons for the abdication of Karl V/Carlos I had much to do with the incredible debt incurred from borrowing two to four million ducats a year. At least six times between 1557 and 1647, the Spanish government went bankrupt, and found itself unable to meet its obligations or to borrow further. These fiscal crises occurred every twenty years with remarkable regularity--1557, 1575, 1596, 1607, 1627, and 1647.

France

From 1437 to the end of the fifteenth century, prices stabilised throughout France. Annual price fluctuations diminished, and the cost of grain remained roughly on the same level for nearly half a century. After 1440, conditions began at last to improve in France. During the reigns of Charles VII and Louis XI, order was restored, the English were defeated and anarchy was suppressed.

As early as 1529, a major famine occurred throughout Europe accompanied by high prices for grain. The two steepest surges of inflation in the 1540s and 1590s were periods of heavy military spending. I have calculated that the peak of French influence was c.1547.

After 1597, France's economic situation improved and agricultural production was aided by milder weather. Henri IV, with his minister Duc de Sully, adopted monetary reforms. Louis XIV's glory was irrevocably linked to two great projects - military conquest and the building of Versailles - both of which required enormous sums of money. Louis XIV's minister of finances, Colbert, started a mercantile system which used protectionism and state-sponsored manufacturing to promote the production of luxury goods over the rest of the economy. Colbert's economic policies were a key element in Louis XIV's creation of a centralised and fortified state and in the promotion of government glory.

The wars and the weather at the end of the century (hot-dry climate peak 1695) brought the economy to the brink: by 1715, the trade deficit had reached 1.1 trillion livres. In 1749, a new tax, modelled on the "*dixième*" and called the "*vingtième*" (or "one-twentieth"), was enacted to reduce the royal deficit. In 1775 the French economy began truly to enter a state of crisis (cold-dry climate peak 1765). An extended reduction in agricultural prices over the previous twelve years, with dramatic crashes in 1777 and 1786, and further complicated by climatic events such as the disastrous winters of 1785-1789 contributed to the problem. Paper money was re-introduced, denominated in livres; these were issued in quantity until 1793 after the French Revolution.

Ottomans

The organization of the treasury and chancery was developed under the Ottoman Empire more than any other Islamic government and, until the 17th century, they were the leading organisation among all their contemporaries. Mehmed II (1444-81) had gold coins *sultani* minted similar to Venetian *ducato* which announced the Ottoman's entry to Europe. He created many trade monopolies which provided much wealth to the treasury.

Islam was not as tolerant towards lending or interest as Christianity. The Holy Koran explicitly forbids usury. Modern Islamic banks still must follow the principles of *Shari'a* which involves capital participation - sharing risk - rather than loans at interest. Turkish merchants obviously had no problems with finance because they were pre-eminent in trade and industry until the sixteenth century.

The Ottoman economy probably reached its zenith in the early sixteenth century because its power stretched between three continents before the Portuguese established direct trade links to India. A financial crisis developed around 1580 from the influx of American silver into Empire. When inflation took off, there were price increases of around 500 percent from the end of the 15th century to the close of the 17th. The *akçe* was devalued 1585-1640. The treasury moved to deficit despite increased taxes.

The Ottoman Empire took its first foreign loans in 1854 during the Crimean War. This major foreign loan was followed by those of 1855, 1858 and 1860, which culminated in default and led to the alienation of European sympathy from Turkey and indirectly to the dethronement and death of Abdul-Aziz in the following years.

Rurik Russia

Ivan III reorganised the land of Rus' in such a way as to impose his power and authority over Muscovy. Among his most important accomplishments was the unification under Moscow of the entire Rus'. Between 1484 and 1505 Ivan III systematically took all the land of Novgorod's aristocracy. He vested the warriors with ample estates in return for devoted military service. By doing this, Ivan planted the first true roots of feudalism in Rus'. Ivan IV's economic legacy was disastrous and contributed to the decline of the Rurik Dynasty and the Time of Troubles.

Safavid Persia

The Silk Road, which led through northern lands to the eastern lands of Persia, revived in the 16th century. Leaders also supported direct trade with Europe, particularly England and the Netherlands, which sought Persian carpet, silk, and textiles. The establishment of a royal monopoly for the export of luxury goods like silk, carpets, and eventually others, governed international trade. Luxury Iranian silk was exchanged for gold and silver, which was in short supply in Iran but plentiful in Europe. Gold and silver coins received from Europe were melted down and re-struck as Iranian dinar coins, which were then used to buy goods from India.

A series of innovations was introduced by Shah Abbās I at the beginning of the 17th century in an attempt to standardise the tax system; they remained in effect until the end of the 18th century. The disintegration of the Safavid Empire was not caused solely by military defeat. The Afghan usurpation should be seen in the context of an economic crisis brought about by royal mismanagement and lack of policy. The collapse of the Safavids provoked a long-term crisis in Persia, not only in the political and military spheres, but also in the economy.

Mughal India

Mughal Emperor Akbar's revenues were from large inflows of foreign silver, imperial control over currency, treasure seized by the ever-conquering empire, and large returns from crown lands. Akbar minted and reminted pure copper, silver and gold coins without charge to those supplying the metal. A central treasury was established, manned mainly by Hindu service castes, to manage salaries and *jagirs*, under supervision of the *wazir* (finance minister) and *bakhshi* (military paymaster).

State incomes doubled from Akbar to Aurangzeb. Aurangzeb's exchequer raised an estimated one billion rupees in annual revenue through various sources like taxes, customs and land revenue etc, from 24 provinces. The agrarian economy expanded, stimulated by the increase in the money supply, growing foreign demand for commodities and textiles, and population growth. Sophisticated systems of credit, insurance and accounting grew to support travelling merchants. At the height of empire in the seventeenth century, monetisation, cultivation of commercial crops and manufactures had enhanced the power of merchants who provided cash and/or credit. Revenues became cumbersome to carry to the imperial centre so the merchants developed the *hundi* (bill of sale) which could be issued at commercial centres for payment at Agra. Sarat was the main Mughal port through which bullion flowed and thus became the financial centre.

From the mid seventeenth century, European fashion discovered chintz, largely from Madras and Pondicherry. The initial demand was for wall-hangings and bed-covers which led to use in clothing. In 1700 when English legislation was passed to prevent imports of dyed or printed cloth, demand grew for unprocessed cotton cloth known as calico. Chintz was still available in England, smuggled from Europe. Throughout the seventeenth and eighteenth centuries there were massive flows of bullion into India –Spanish silver from European markets; African and Japanese gold – in exchange for Indian products. These supplies allowed the monetisation of the Indian economy.

As the empire disintegrated, traders left Agra and travel between Surat and Agra became hazardous. Bankers in Surat refused to issue *hundis* for Agra. The independence of the Punjab and the strength of Afghan tribes led to disruptions to one of India's manufacturing centres. The waning of imperial power led to a recession in the north. From the mid eighteenth century Mughal coffers were virtually empty.

Ming China

The Ming saw the rise of commercial plantations that produced crops suitable to their regions of China. Tea, fruits, and other goods were produced on a massive scale by these agricultural plantations. Regional patterns of production established during this period continued into the Qing dynasty. The Columbian exchange brought crops such as corn with these foreign crops. During the Ming, specialised areas also popped up planting large numbers of cash crops that could be sold at markets. Large numbers of peasants abandoned the land to become artisans. The population of the Ming boomed; estimates for the population of the Ming range from 160 to 200 million.

The Ming dynasty also engaged in a thriving trade with both Europe and Japan. Chinese silver mines were exhausted in the 1530s. This nearly coincided with a glut of silver in Europe from American silver mines. Increasing quantities of silver were imported largely from Latin America through the Philippines, which later led to the use of the Spanish Carolus peso as a common form of currency. In addition to silver, the Ming also imported many European firearms, in order to ensure the modernity of their weapons. The gentry and merchant classes started to fuse, and the merchants gained power at the expense of the state.

With the coming of the Little Ice Age in the 17th century, the state's low revenues and its inability to raise taxes caused massive deficits, and large numbers of Ming troops defected or rebelled because they had not been paid. Many Chinese scholars believe the Ming was the dynasty in which the "sprouts of capitalism" emerged in China, only to be suppressed by the Qing.

Holland

The Dutch East India Company (*Vereenigde Oost-Indische Compagnie, VOC*) was established in 1602 with a 21-year monopoly to carry out colonial activities in Asia. It was arguably the world's first mega-corporation, possessing quasi-governmental powers, including the ability to wage war, imprison and execute convicts, negotiate treaties, coin money, and establish colonies. By 1669 the VOC was the richest company in the world controlling 150+ merchant ships, 40 warships and a private army of 10,000 soldiers. With 50,000 employees, the company paid a dividend of 40% of the original investment. Between 1602 and

1796 the VOC sent almost a million Europeans to work in the Asia trade on 4,785 ships, and netted for their efforts more than 2.5 million tons of Asian trade goods.

The Dutch West India Company (*Geoctroyeerde Westindische Compagnie, WIC*) was garnted a charter in 1621 for a trade monopoly of 24 years in the West Indies. When the plan to seize Portuguese colonies failed, privateering became one of the major goals within the WIC. The company was initially relatively successful; in the 1620s and 1630s, many trade posts or colonies were established. The New Netherland area, which included New Amsterdam, covered parts of present-day New York, Connecticut, Delaware, and New Jersey. Other settlements were established on the Netherlands Antilles, several other Caribbean islands, Suriname and Guyana. Because of the ongoing war in Brazil the situation for the WIC in 1645, at the end of the charter, was very bad. After years of debt, the WIC was reformed in 1674 to concentrate on the slave trade and eventual failure in the eighteenth century.

Amsterdam developed a "*stapelmarkt*" where goods could be stored temporarily for re-export. This allowed traders to offer and bid for commodities in a free market according to supply and demand. The large influx of immigrants from Antwerp and Portugal (Jews) brought a rapid accumulation of trade capital. The need of governments to raise funds for expensive wars once again gave rise to reliance on money-lenders, although in the sophisticated seventeenth century, financiers provided long term public debt rather than the physical Italian coins of the past. The new financial instruments could be traded on the Amsterdam Stock Exchange thus spreading the risk of any default. The *Amsterdamsche Wisselbank*, also called the Bank of Amsterdam, was established in 1609. Insurance was formalised as a contractual business, first offered by merchants as part of their normal trade, later by specialised insurers. This type of business started with marine insurance. In 1598 (three years before a similar institution was established in England) the city of Amsterdam instituted a *Kamer van Assurantie en Avarij* (Chamber of Marine Insurance) which was charged with regulating this business.

Unfortunately, 1632 proved from hindsight to be a top year for property prices. As rents plunged after the middle of the century, the real burden of the *verponding* (property tax) therefore increased sharply. Trading for quick profits continued as normal in Amsterdam during the revolution. In fact, such was the appetite for trading risk that a boom occurred in the price of tulips and the bust resulted in the world's first known stock market crash.

There was a sharp break in the economy after 1672. Whereas the economy stagnated, expenditures in connection with the wars, and hence taxes too, rose. Taxes doubled by the 1690s, but nominal wages (as distinguished from real wages, which rose due to the general decline in price levels) remained constant. At the same time the tax base almost certainly shrank as a consequence of the economic decline. This resulted in a doubling of the *per-capita* tax burden. This development levelled off after the Peace of Utrecht in 1713, when the Republic entered a period of peace and neutrality. As by the end of the 17th century, structural problems in the Dutch economy precluded profitable investment of this capital in domestic Dutch sectors, the stream of investments was redirected more and more to investment abroad, both in sovereign debt and foreign stocks, bonds and infrastructure. The Netherlands came to dominate the international capital market up to the crises of the end of the 18th century that caused the demise of the Dutch Republic.

Japan

Until the Tokugawa Shogunate, Japan was dependent on Chinese bronze coins for its currency. Tokugawa coinage worked according to a triple monetary standard, using gold, silver and bronze coins, each with their own denominations. In 1588 Hideyoshi introduced the unwieldy gold *oban* plate worth ten Ryo. Increased agricultural growth in peace created growth in trade which in turn created a need for proper currency. Tokugawa Ietsugu introduced in 1714 with the introduction of a new Koban and an Ichibuban (both 86%gold 14%silver). An export ban on monetary specie was imposed by Arai Hakuseki in 1715.

Tokugawa Yoshimune instituted a series of economic reforms in the 1730s and 1740s. Currency reform included the shift to hard money from rice as a medium of exchange, and debasement of coins. The reforms were ineffective in solving the financial position of the *bakufu*, the impoverishment of *samurai* and the accumulation of wealth by the merchant class. In 1736 deflation forced an increase in the money supply. From 1772 silver coins were issued as fiduciary coinage without face value weight of silver.

The Japanese monetary system was sufficient for the country's needs in isolation but when foreign trade was forced on the government, the demand for foreign goods brought high inflation. The price of rice increased fourfold from 1853 to 1869. The 1715 embargo on export of bullion was effectively lifted, which caused a massive outflow of gold as foreigners swapped silver for undervalued gold. The government responded by debasing the gold content of its coins by two-thirds to match international gold-silver exchange rates.

Prussia/Germany

During the reign of Friedrich II, the effects of the Seven Years' War and the gaining of Silesia greatly changed the economy. The Fifth Department of the General Directory was tasked with overseeing commerce and manufacturing. Prussian colonisation agencies opened in Hamburg, Frankfurt/Main, Regensburg, Amsterdam and Geneva. Wool spinners were recruited to provide Prussia wool manufacturers with labour, and skilled labourers were enticed to work in Prussian silk factories. Immigrants founded factories manufacturing knives and scissors and helped build hat and leather industries. There was a royal shipyard at Stettin and government monopolies in tobacco, timber, coffee and salt operated by businessmen under government supervision. In 1753 the first German ironworks to operate a blast furnace, opened.

The circulation of depreciated money kept prices high. To revalue the Thaler, the Mint Edict of May 1763 was proposed. This stabilised the rates of depreciated coins that would not be accepted and provided for the payments of taxes in currency of pre-war value. This was replaced in northern Germany by the *Reichsthaler*, worth one-fourth of a Conventions thaler. Prussia used a Thaler containing one-fourteenth of a Cologne mark of silver. Many other rulers soon followed the steps of Friedrich in reforming their own currencies—this resulted in a shortage of ready money thus lowering prices.

The Panic of 1837 triggered by the failing banks in America was followed by a severe depression lasting until 1845. In the mid-1840s several harvests failed across Europe, which caused famines.

During the 1850s and 1860s, the Prussian economy experienced the transforming effects of the first world boom. Rapid growth in the railway network and in associated enterprises, such as steel smelting and machine construction, was supported by a great expansion in the extraction of fossil fuels. The coalmines in the Ruhr of the Prussian Rhineland increased rapidly in the 1860s bringing rapid economic and social change. There was a liquid capital market (assisted by gold rushes in Australia and California), favourable balance of trade and cutting of Prussia government red-tape. The 1860s witnessed a coordinated expansion across heavy industry, textile and agriculture, and investment through banks and joint-stock companies.

In 1873, Germany and much of Europe and America entered the Long Depression, (*Gründerkrise*). A downturn hit the German economy for the first time since industrial development began the surge that followed the post-unification speculative bubble. To aid faltering industries, the Chancellor abandoned free trade and established protectionist tariffs (taxes on imports), which alienated the National Liberals who demanded free trade.

German banks played central roles in financing German industry. Different banks formed cartels in different industries. Cartel contracts were accepted as legal and binding by German courts although they were held to be illegal in Britain and the United States.

The process of cartelisation began slowly, but the cartel movement took hold after 1873 in the economic depression. It began in heavy industry and spread throughout other industries. By 1900 there were 275 cartels in operation; by 1908, over 500. By some estimates, different cartel arrangements may have numbered in the thousands at different times, but many German companies stayed outside the cartels because they did not welcome the restrictions that membership imposed.

Germany became Europe's leading steel producing nation in the late 19th century, thanks in large part to the protection from American and British competition afforded by tariffs and cartels. The government played a powerful role in the industrialisation of the German Empire. It supported not only heavy industry but also crafts and trades because it wanted to maintain prosperity in all parts of the empire. Even where the national government did not act, the highly autonomous regional and local governments supported their own industries. Each state tried to be as self-sufficient as possible.

The common factor of cultures under review was that the regime declined when debt was contracted to support the economy.

Advances in Technology

Of great importance to Europe of the Habsburgs was the invention of new print technology. Johannes Gutenberg published his Latin edition of the Bible in Mainz in 1450. The popularity of the printed book cause publishing houses to spring up throughout Europe. By 1475 most of the classic works in Latin were available in print. By 1500 it is estimated that 20 million volumes had been produced, enough for one person in five to own a book in largely illiterate Europe.

Spanish captain Gonzalo Fernandez de Cordoba introduced the combination of arquebus and pike. Spain made few innovations in the design and operation of their ships. Caravels and galleons were adaptations of earlier European largely Portuguese designs. The success of English privateers caused changes to Spanish ships along English lines. Navigation was by charts and astrolabe, largely copied from the Portuguese in turn influenced by Genoa.

In 1494 artificers of France King Charles VIII solved an artillery problem by producing field guns with a two-wheel carriage capable of elevation. The French led in developing high quality culverins along with the gun carriage with the high wheels and long tail that defined artillery pieces until the nineteenth century. The wheel-lock pistol, introduced in the 16th century, was far more expensive to make than the arquebus, and its expense restricted its use to those who could afford it—the nobles. During the French Wars of Religion (1561-1598), pistoleers came to make up most of the French mounted troops, and the knights disappeared. Claude-Étienne Minié invented the Minié rifle following the invention of the Minié ball in 1847. The Minié ball was a conical-cylindrical soft lead bullet designed to expand under the pressure and obdurate the barrel and increase muzzle velocity of the spin-stabilised rifle bullet. The Chassepot, officially known as *Fusil modèle 1866*, was a bolt action military breech loading rifle, famous as the arm of the French forces in the Franco-Prussian War of 1870-1871. It replaced an assortment of Minié muzzle loading rifles.

The Ottoman army was one of the first forces in the world to use muskets and cannons. Short wide cannons (falconets) were used during the Siege of Constantinople 1422. Technology then produced three enormous 25inch cannon for the Siege of Constantinople in 1453. One of the greatest advancements in Ottoman fire arms came in the reign of Bayezid II (1481-1512) who improved the design of field artillery pieces and many other firearms ranging from muskets to *tufeks* (arquebus). To add to this, the 16th century brought the latest technical advancements in gun making to the Ottomans; in the form of Jews fleeing from the Spanish Inquisition. Taqi al-Din (1526-1585) is known for the invention of a six-cylinder '*Monobloc*' pump in 1559, the invention of a variety of accurate clocks (including the first mechanical alarm clock, the first spring-powered astronomical clock, the first watch measured in minutes and the first clocks measured in minutes and seconds) from 1556 to 1580, the possible invention of an early telescope 1574.

After the defeat at Vienna 1683 the *Sublime Porte* (central government) realised that military technology transfer was again necessary. Military officers were trained in European warfare and equipped with the same type of weapons as European armies. Modernisation was then resisted by the Janissaries whose decline was reflected in the fall of empire.

During 1657, the Mughals are known to have utilised rockets during the Siege of Bidar. Mughal cannon production reached its zenith during the reign of Aurangzeb. Until the later part of the seventeenth century, such manufacture in India was principally the work of Europeans, with indigenous workers gradually assimilating their skills. Later, the Mysorean rockets were upgraded versions of Mughal rockets utilised during the Siege of Jinji by the progeny of the Nawab of Arcot. Hyder Ali realised the importance of rockets and introduced advanced versions of metal cylinder rockets. These rockets turned fortunes in favour of the Sultanate of Mysore during the Second Anglo-Mysore War (1780-84) particularly during the Battle of Pollilur. As often happens with dominant cultures, technology was mainly introduced and not Indian inventions.

The Ming Chinese were intrigued with European technology, but so were visiting Europeans of Chinese technology. The encyclopaedist Song Yingxing (1587–1666) documented a wide array of technologies, metallurgic and industrial processes in his *Tiangong Kaiwu* encyclopaedia of 1637. This includes mechanical and hydraulic powered devices for agriculture and irrigation, nautical technology such as vessel types and snorkelling gear for pearl divers, the annual processes of sericulture and weaving with the loom, metallurgic processes such as the crucible technique and quenching, manufacturing processes such as for roasting iron pyrites in converting sulphide to oxide in sulphur used in gunpowder compositions and the use of gunpowder weapons such as a naval mine ignited by use of a rip-cord and steel flint wheel. The early Ming period featured many types of cutting-edge gunpowder weaponry for the time. There were many advances and new designs in gunpowder weapons during the beginning of the dynasty, but by the mid to late Ming the Chinese began to frequently employ European-style artillery and firearms.

The long term future of the Dutch Republic was secured by an explosion of economic growth and a technological revolution in shipbuilding. Trading ships were designed by merchants who produced the *fluyt* (flyboat), a long shallow draft ship without heavy weapons that made extensive use of the block and tackle to reduce crew members. The relatively cheap *fluyt* provided the basis for Dutch mercantile trade. Dutch bankers were innovators in financial engineering.

The Japanese had used basic firearms and cannon tubes introduced from China since the thirteenth century. It is thought that Portuguese traders introduced light hand guns, arquebus, with a matchlock firing mechanism to the Japanese southern island of Tanegashima c.1543 during the Sengoku period of civil war. Japanese swordsmiths and ironsmiths managed to replicate the matchlock mechanism and soon were able to mass-produce copies of the Portuguese guns.

The Prussians employed rigorously testing and modifying the Dreyse prototype of needle-gun with the result that its specifications steadily improved over successive batches, while costs of production and ammunition fell. The rifle was the invention of the gunsmith Johann Nikolaus von Dreyse (1787–1867) who, in 1836 produced the complete needle-gun. Dreyse was ennobled in 1864

Conclusion – the Cyclical Pattern Continues

The pattern of early Capitalist-era dominant societies shows a rhythm similar in phase with those of past cultures. The above cultures were lead by monarchs, emperors and generals which produced similar patterns identified in my ancient and medieval research. When dynasties weakened and/or rulers were unable to govern their bureaucracy the culture was weakened and dominance slowly diminished.

The real test of the long term cyclical theory of human progress will occur in following chapters when democratic forms of government replace sole rulers. It is my theory that even sole rulers were influenced by the mass behaviour of their subjects, so that cycles should become more apparent when directly influenced by democratic principles, demonstrated by the British Empire and the Republic of the United States of America.

INDEX

K

Karl V   69, 71, 77-8, 113, 115, 118
Kashmir   63
King, M.L.   34, 42-5, 47-8, 52-5, 58, 65,
    69, 71, 74-6, 78-9, 82-3, 86-9, 100-
    1, 103-7, 109
Komei   95-6
Kondratieff N.D.   30
Koran   113, 119

L

Lee, R.E. General   15
Longqing   68
Louis XI   63, 76, 118
Louis XII   76-7
Louis XIII   79
Louis XIV   79-82, 100, 114, 119
Louis XVI   83-4

M

Madras   86, 121
Malacca   64
Manchu   69, 98
Maria de Medici   79
Marie Stuart   78
Marx K   31
Maximilian I   62
Mazarin   79-80
Mehmed II   62, 70, 116, 119
Mehmed III   71
Mehmed IV   72
Meiji   96
Mills C.A.   27

Ming   62, 66, 68-9, 91, 98, 112, 115, 122,
    128
Mississippi Bubble   32
Moltke   107
Mongolia   67
Montesquieu, C.L.   26-7
Moscow   62, 65-6, 120
Mughal   63, 73, 84-9, 116, 121, 128
Murad II   70
Murad III   71
Murad IV   72
Muscovy   62, 65-6, 115, 120
Muslim   37-8, 40, 43, 51, 54, 58, 63, 70-1,
    73-5, 85, 112-14, 116

N

Nanking   66
National Debt   80
Nazi   111
Netherlands   69-70, 78, 81-2, 97, 99, 111,
    118, 120, 123-4
New Zealand   23
Nobunaga   64, 90
North, F.   15, 20-1, 27, 40-1, 44, 57, 62-4,
    67, 79, 82, 87-8, 96, 118, 121

O

opium   75, 84-5
Orthodox   8, 43, 47-8, 71, 112
Osaka   91-3
Ottoman   39, 62, 70-4, 77, 103, 113, 116,
    119-20, 127